KOREA MIRACLE

Korea Miracle

COLIN WHITTAKER

KINGSWAY PUBLICATIONS
EASTBOURNE

Copyright © Colin Whittaker 1988

First Published 1988

Front cover design by Vic Mitchell

British Library Cataloguing in Publication Data

Whittaker, Colin
  Korea miracle.
  1. Korea. Christian church, to 1988
  I. Title
  275.19

  ISBN 0–86065–522–9

Printed in Great Britain for
KINGSWAY PUBLICATIONS LTD
Lottbridge Drove, Eastbourne, E Sussex BN23 6NT by
Richard Clay Ltd, Bungay, Suffolk.
Typeset by Nuprint Ltd, Harpenden, Herts AL5 4SE

Contents

Preface

The longer I live, the more I appreciate that God's timing is perfect. To be honest, though, I seldom feel that way at the time. It is usually only in retrospect that I realise this to be so.

The trip to Korea was very much a case in point. When Kingsway approached me about writing a book on the revival in Korea, I was thrilled beyond measure. It was a dream come true! I cheerfully confess that my interest in revival amounts almost to an obsession. The opportunity, therefore, to visit this small Far Eastern country where the Spirit of God has been moving so wonderfully over the past thirty-five years, to investigate and report on the phenomenon, was I believed 'heaven sent'. It was a special joy to know that my dear wife, Hazel, who has shared thirty-seven years in the ministry with me, was going to be able to accompany me on the trip. Both of us share a long and ongoing interest in prayer, and the prospect of visiting some of Korea's prayer mountains and participating in their all-nights of prayer delighted us.

As we prayerfully planned the trip—writing to Korea, finding out such things as when Yonggi Cho would be in Seoul and available for interviews, booking flights, arranging for a fairly long absence from our own church in Bristol, and all the other preparations for such an undertaking—we had a calm assurance that we were moving in the will of God. Everything seemed to be working out perfectly.

The flying time to Korea is more than twenty-four hours. Since we travelled economy class on a packed plane, we were tired by the time we disembarked that June evening at the much publicised Kimpo International Airport on the outskirts of Seoul. Even so, our fatigue and stiffness were quickly forgotten in the thrill of arriving in Korea. Our luggage was the very last to appear on the carousel, which made us the last in the long, long queues at customs. We comforted ourselves that it would not take long to get through — after all, we had 'nothing to declare'. But that notion vanished after a few minutes, when we saw that the customs men were opening and searching every single piece of luggage belonging to every person — whichever gate they were going through. As we looked around the airport we saw armed guards and realised there was a sense of emergency in the air. The day we arrived in Korea in early June 1987 was the day the student demonstrations began. The day we left was the day the riots and demonstrations subsided. Talk about timing . . .

Because we lacked English-language newspapers and radio programmes, we remained in blissful ignorance for our first two days of the serious trouble that was brewing on the streets of Seoul with the student demonstrations. We decided to visit the centre of Seoul and hailed a taxi without any difficulty and without too much expense. The taxi dropped us where we requested, but within seconds Hazel was dabbing her eyes. We were passing a building site and I thought it was building dust, but a few minutes later the truth dawned that it was tear gas. We had arrived almost at the epicentre of the student demonstrations, which had been going on all night. Timing? — we certainly did not want to talk about timing then.

Though the tear gas lingering in the air made things unpleasant, with everyone dabbing their eyes and sneezing as though it was a flu epidemic, otherwise life seemed to be carrying on pretty much as normal — so we decided to do the same. It was only when we phoned our daughter in England that we realised just what was going on in Seoul. She was quite alarmed for us, as the pictures on British television and the reports in the newspapers were making the headlines. We assured her that we were quite safe and not to worry. Nevertheless, next day we decided to keep away from the parts of the city centre where the main troubles seemed to be. Instead, we opted to confine our immediate excursions to Yoido island, where the Full Gospel Church pastored by Yonggi Cho is situated and where we were staying.

We visited the Dae Han Life Insurance Building, claimed to be the highest building in South East Asia, with sixty-three storeys. The head of the corporation is a Christian. The magnificent structure in gold-coloured glass dominates the Han River area and is most impressive. On the ground floor there is a modern shopping complex and — would you believe it? — an American-style fast food centre, with half-a-dozen different areas supplying everything from hamburgers to pizzas, from ice-cream to doughnuts. In the complex are also the Korean, Japanese and Chinese restaurants one would expect.

We felt secure in this environment, until suddenly the lights dimmed, everything closed up, and everyone gathered around television sets which were located in a number of places in the eating areas. Up until then these had been showing normal programmes (in Korean, of course, but there was soccer on most screens and that is the same in any language). We discovered we were the only ones standing, so we decided to sit down like the rest. The television sets all started showing another programme. Even without any knowledge of Korean it was obvious what it was. It was a propaganda war preparation film — and it immediately brought back memories of the Ministry of Information films which had become all too familiar to us in Britain back in 1939 and 1940. The commentary in Korean went over our heads, but the graphic pictures of air raids and soldiers in action and first aid were readily understood. We soon realised that some shots were from the Korean War of 1950–3, and much of it concerned the danger of another attack from North Korea. It ran for about half an hour, then the lights came on again, the restaurants and shops reopened and everyone carried on normally—to our huge relief. We found that not many Koreans speak English, and very few indeed know sufficient English to hold the kind of conversation needed to answer 'What is going on here? Could you please tell us?'

We wandered around the magnificent building for a little while feeling rather disturbed, a sensation which was heightened, of course, by our ignorance of the language. There is an express lift to the top floor, where there is a viewing area from which one can get a marvellous panoramic view of the vast, sprawling city of Seoul—the seventh-largest city in the world today, with a population fast approaching ten million, and with over 2,000 Christian churches. The express lift is the fastest we have ever travelled on, and if you choose to ascend by the viewing lift, which is glass and situated on the outside of the building, it is quite an experience.

We returned to our sixth-floor accommodation in the fourteen-storey Education Building adjoining the 25,000-seater Yoido Full Gospel Church. Among so many praying people, what could possibly happen? We got into the lift, and a little girl aged about ten or eleven years and obviously mentally handicapped got in at the same time. Yonggi Cho's church carries out a lot of social work, including special care and help for mentally handicapped children. We pressed the button for the sixth floor and the lift ascended, until suddenly about midway between the fourth and fifth floors it stopped and the light went out, leaving us stuck in total darkness and with this little

handicapped girl. Fortunately she did not panic—we did
that! With the war film still fresh in our minds, our
imaginations ran riot. We fumbled for the emergency
button and called out for help. After what seemed like a
millennium but was in reality only a few minutes, Hazel
located the emergency button and a voice responded in
Korean. They eventually got the lift restarted and we
emerged rather shaken and seriously wondering, 'Have
we really come to the Korean "kingdom" for such a time
as this?'

For a few days things did seem to be going wrong:
hoped-for interviews were not forthcoming, the language
was proving a real obstacle, and so on. But then one after
the other, friends were made, help appeared from many
sources, and everything slotted into place. At the end of
our stay we felt sure that God's timing had been perfect
after all. The emergency situation had served to bring to
the surface the hidden tensions and problems of Korea,
so that we gained insights which we would certainly have
missed if we had come at a more 'normal time'.

We became good friends with four postgraduate
students from Oral Roberts University, Tulsa, USA. They
were the first students to be brought over on a special
scheme run by Yonggi Cho's Church Growth International. Their main task was to study the cell group
system, and they were each assigned to a different district.
These fine young men with typical American generosity
shared freely all their findings, which was an invaluable
help. God had provided us with a whole research team.
Thank you, 'magnificent four': William E Boylan, David
H Hay, James D Marks and Ed Lingren. Best of all, they
all spoke English—well, nearly! Indeed, I was mystified
as to why any Koreans who had a little English seemed
to understand the Americans better than they did me.
One day, however, I was in the Yoido Church's Bible
Institute and talking with the Director, Yong Chan Cho,
a brother of Yonggi Cho. As we were discussing the

curriculum of the Institute, I noticed on his desk a textbook: *American Hollywood English for Korean Students*. The
mystery was solved and my pride somewhat mollified.

All the people at Yoido Full Gospel Church seemed so
busy that it was difficult to arrange interviews; I began
to wonder whether they had discovered the secret of
perpetual motion. However, the ones that really mattered
did eventually stop and were more than helpful and
generous with their time, especially Dr Paul Yonggi Cho
himself, who gave me personal interviews and instructed
his staff to help in every way possible. His personal
secretary, Mrs Lydia Swain, was so very patient and kind
to us and gave us such a wealth of material. She and
her husband and their young family came to Korea as
missionaries from American Assemblies of God in 1964,
and apart from a brief spell in Thailand spent all their
missionary service in Korea, much of it working with
Yonggi Cho. Her husband caught a fatal infection when
helping people in a disaster area in Thailand at the beginning of the 1980s. Mrs Swain is now an invaluable help
in her present vital role. We owe so much to her for her
assistance, fellowship, and for arranging so many
interviews.

What more can I say? We were privileged to meet and
interview so many key people. There was Dr Jashil Choi,
Yonggi Cho's mother-in-law and the lady responsible for
bringing Prayer Mountain into being. Also, a host of
other marvellous people on the staff at Yoido Full Gospel
Church, including the two Miss Lees: one was Mrs
Swain's secretary and an excellent interpreter for us, the
other was the Secretary in the very busy Church Growth
International Centre. In spite of being so busy, preparing
for the eighth Church Growth International Conference
in the World Mission Centre, with such distinguished
guests as Peter Wagner, Robert Schuller, Larry Lea and
Reg Klimionock (to name but four from a whole galaxy

of international speakers), the second Miss Lee did finally squeeze in an interview with me.

Outside Yoido Full Gospel Church we were also privileged to interview so many great people, such as Dr Marlin L Nelson, Professor of Missions at the very important and interesting Asia Centre for Theological Studies and Missions. Dr Nelson is another example from the army of outstanding missionaries who have given the best years of their lives to Korea. His insights into the Korean church as a whole were a unique contribution to our research. The book he edited along with Bong-Rin Ro specially for the centennial of the Protestant Church in Korea (1884–1984), entitled *Korean Church Growth Explosion* and published by Word of Life Press, Asia Theological Association, is a must for anyone interested in further reading on the Korean church. Korea is living proof that missionary work is not in vain. Korean church leaders are the first to acknowledge their debt to the missionaries from many societies who have played such a vital part in establishing the Christian faith in what was a totally alien culture.

Other names cry out to be mentioned in this preface, such as the Revd Dr Kim Sun-Do, the senior minister of Kwang Lim Methodist Church, the largest Methodist church in the world, who gave us so generously of his time. There are others, dozens of rank-and-file Korean Christians who talked to us and blessed us and helped us to a new appreciation of God's grace and love as we saw Christianity working at the grass roots of their society.

Once again I have to thank my dear wife Hazel, who on this trip, as throughout our married life, was such a marvellous help, absolutely indispensable: sharing notes together, helping to tape many of the interviews, and her special part in our meeting so many Christian women, which would have been difficult, if not impossible, had I been alone. The other woman in my life who has also made herself indispensable in my writing ministry is my older married daughter Beryl, who once again has done her school-teacher role and 'marked' my manuscript for me. She tells me I am improving!

Miracle is a much overworked word these days in Christian circles, but I trust that reading this book and seeing a little of what God has done and is doing in this great little country, you will agree that it is a miracle. I have endeavoured to fulfil the mandate given me by Kingsway in telling the story of the revival in Korea. It is impossible to appreciate what is happening in the present without a brief survey of the past; this I have tried to keep to the minimum necessary for a balanced and realistic appraisal.

Kingsway said they wanted this to be a companion book to my good friend Arthur Wallis's *China Miracle*. Our styles are different and the two countries could not be more of a contrast—not only in size but in just about every way—but both provide up-to-date evidence of God at work today in the world. Yonggi Cho and other Korean church leaders believe that God in his infinite wisdom has allowed Korea to be one of the last countries to receive the gospel because he has for it a very special purpose: to make it an example of a Christian nation, wholly committed to him and to world evangelism. God's timing is perfect and Korea is another proof of it. Korea is a miracle.

After visiting Korea one can only bow one's head and wonder and worship and declare with Paul: 'O the depth of the riches both of the wisdom and knowledge of God! how unsearchable are his judgments, and his ways past finding out!' (Rom 11:33).

I

The Miracle of a Prepared People

The Koreans are a unique race and the modern world is being made increasingly aware of the fact. For example, groups of young Koreans fought against the communists in Vietnam. They soon gained such a reputation for their determination that the Reds issued a directive to their men: 'Never touch a Korean unit unless you are absolutely sure of success.'

That same determined spirit can be seen in the regular routine of Korean church life, where all-nights of prayer are the norm for millions of believers. It cannot be coincidence that the world's largest Methodist church, Presbyterian church and Pentecostal church are all to be found in Korea's capital city of Seoul. Nor can it be by chance that every Friday all three churches have nights of prayer which are attended by thousands. Neither does it just happen that the Pentecostal church, which is the biggest church in the world with over half a million members, has an all-night of prayer every single night of the week. The smallest of these prayer gatherings is attended by around two thousand people and the biggest by over twenty thousand.

Again and again the Devil has moved to destroy the comparatively young Korean church, which only celebrated its centenary in 1984. Its short but action-packed history is one of such suffering that its very survival is astonishing, and its outstanding growth in the face of overwhelming opposition is nothing short of miraculous. It is probably not stretching the bounds of imagination too far to think that the powers of darkness have also been ordered not to touch the Korean church again unless they can be absolutely sure of success!

In many ways the story of the growth of the Christian church in Korea stands in direct contrast to that of the church in China. Korea is one of the smallest nations and countries; China is the largest nation and one of the biggest countries. In Korea the church is very much out in the open: highly organised, involved in every aspect of the nation's life, erecting magnificent buildings, and using the latest technologies from computers to television. In China the church is still mainly underground and hidden because of the repressive communist regime. It has no buildings, virtually no organisation, and is denied the use of any modern technology.

Yet both Korea and China are experiencing amazing church growth which shows no sign of abating. Both are constantly seeing signs and wonders of the kind which would set Dr Luke's pen itching to add a few more chapters to Acts. Both pray with a commitment and faith which shames the affluent but apathetic Western Church. Indeed, Korean Christians who have visited the West will readily tell you that they feel that our praying is passive whilst theirs is aggressive. They expect answers, and in the main they get them. We, on the other hand, don't really expect answers to many of our prayers and are usually more surprised when they do come than when they don't! We wrap up our unanswered prayers with phrases such as: 'Oh well, it can't have been God's will.' They are more sure of God's will before they start praying and much more determined to persist until a definite answer is obtained.

This attitude of 'praying through' seems to be ingrained in Korean Christians even when they go to live abroad.

Whilst we were in Yonggi Cho's mega-church, the Pente-costal Yoido Full Gospel Church, we were asked if we knew anything about the International Bible Training Institute in Burgess Hill, Sussex, England, as one of their young ladies had gone there to study. We were able to reassure them that it was a Pentecostal college with an excellent reputation, and that a fine young man from our church was also studying there. On our return to England we asked him if he knew this young lady, and he told us of the impact she had had on the college. From the first she had set herself to pray for the conversion of her non-Christian parents; she had a definite faith that they would both be converted whilst she was at college. She was delighted but apparently not unduly surprised when she received the news of her parents' salvation. It was an object lesson on prayer power to the 'watching and wondering' European students. Korean Christians have much to teach us on the secrets of prayer, and I have endeavoured to weave as much as possible of what we learned about it into the pages of this book.

If their ordinary praying does not produce an answer, then their next resort is usually to go to their church's prayer mountain and give themselves to seeking God by praying and fasting for a week or more. After a week of such devotional concentration, many chronic cases of all kinds are healed or delivered, and many pray through to an assurance that their unsaved families will soon be yielding their lives to Christ. Fasting is a regular feature of Christian living in Korea. It is the key to many difficult situations. Dr Paul Yonggi Cho, is the pastor of Yoido Full Gospel Church in Seoul, which with over 530,000 members is, as I said, the largest church in the world. He told me that if he has a problem with one of his young pastors (and with several hundred of them on his staff, this is inevitable from time to time), he usually despatches him to the church's prayer mountain with orders to pray and fast and seek the face of God for seven or ten days.

Almost without fail, apparently, they return restored and renewed in their faith and zeal for God.

Praying has top priority with Korean Christians, whereas in the West we have allowed prayer to slip almost to the bottom of our church programmes. Neglect of prayer is the reason behind many a tragic fall into temptation of Christian leaders. Take, for instance, the sad scandal of the downfall of the television evangelist Jimmy Bakker, which was rocking the Christian world at the time we were in Korea gathering material for this book. Pastor Yonggi Cho is no stranger to the pressures and temptations which are part and parcel of success in television. It is very much a case of 'watch and pray'. He has learned to use television as an effective medium for proclaiming the gospel, not only throughout his own country but also in Japan as a great missionary means of reaching that nation of viewer addicts, and also right across America where he receives top ratings. The secret lies in the fervent praying of all concerned in producing his programmes. One of his television team used to work for Jimmy Bakker's *Praise the Lord* programme. This man told Yonggi Cho that there was no prayer among the crew and production personnel before or after Bakker's show, but he was immediately conscious of the difference when he switched to working for Cho, where everyone engaged in much earnest intercession before and after each telecast. Without the safeguard of constant prayer it is all too easy for all preachers, not only television evangelists, to lapse into being simply actors.

Until nearly the end of the nineteenth century, Korea was known as 'the hermit nation'. Korea is a peninsula perched perilously on the eastern side of the great mainlands of China and Russia: a little appendix and a constant irritation to both nations, yet it has resisted all their political operations to take it over. In addition, the ever-voracious yellow tiger of Japan lies, licking its lips, just a few hundred miles to the south across the Korea

Straits, waiting for an opportunity to pounce and devour its small neighbour.

The beginning of this proud and ancient nation of Korea dates back to over two thousand years before Christ. From time to time all its larger neighbours have invaded, but their attempts to assimilate it have failed. To this day South Korea remains one people with one common language. Daily the millions of Christians in South Korea pray for the spiritual conversion and political liberation of the twenty million of their fellow countrymen who are trapped behind the 38th parallel, in communist North Korea. They believe God will answer their prayers, which they back up with gospel broadcasts over the border. Every so often a few hardy souls risk life and limb to escape from the oppressive and fanatical Red regime of the North to the comparative, if troubled, freedom of the Republic of Korea in the South.

Today, South Korea is flourishing economically and spiritually. Along with Israel and Taiwan, South Korea has the world's fastest-growing economy and greatest level of industrialisation. However, it is absolutely unique in that spiritually it is prospering even more, and is fast becoming one of the most Christian nations on earth. All this in spite of the fact that this 'hermit nation' had to be virtually dragged, kicking and screaming after centuries of seclusion, into the twentieth century.

Korea embraced three main religions in the course of its long history. The oldest is Shamanism, a form of spirit worship, with gods, demons and demi-gods, and idols, and this remains the most common religion today. Then came Buddhism in the fourth century AD, followed around the sixth century by Confucianism. Strictly speaking, Confucianism is not a religion, but in time it became one to all intents and purposes. The early attempts to introduce Christianity into Korea were vigorously repulsed, and some two hundred years ago caused the first Catholic missionaries and many of their converts to pay the price of martyrdom. The story was repeated just over one hundred years ago with the deaths of the first Protestant missionaries and many of their followers. To be caught with a Bible in those perilous times was enough to cost you your life. At great personal risk, Bibles were smuggled in (who said Bible smuggling was new?) until a new day of freedom dawned.

The Korea miracle is an amazing story, and because it has happened within the compass of the last hundred years, its many lessons are there to be seen. In essence it is the story of a great revival which occurred in 1907. In that event the Holy Spirit successfully grafted Christianity into Korean culture in such a way that Christianity was no longer 'a foreigners' religion' but one which truly belonged to Korea as a nation. Tribute for this must be paid to the first missionaries who set out to establish an indigenous church on New Testament principles.

How the infant church survived the forty cruel years of Japanese occupation is a part of the story which must be told if the miracle of today's Korean church growth is to be appreciated in full. The blood of the martyr is the seed of the church, and there were plenty of them to provide the seed during those troubled years of oppression. The great day of liberation from the Japanese finally came with the Allies' victory over Japan in 1945, but the relief was short-lived, for the Allies divided the country into North and South by the 38th parallel, with the Russians occupying the North and the Americans the South.

Five uneasy years of peace were shattered on the Sunday morning of 25th June 1950 when the new and extreme communist government of North Korea, without warning invaded South Korea. The North Koreans were confident that they could take the whole country before the Americans and the United Nations could mobilise their armies—and they very nearly succeeded. The bloody conflict of the Korean War is indelibly etched in the memories of the relatives of the dead of some sixteen nations (including Britain and many Commonwealth countries as well as America), all of whom rallied to the cause and finally pushed the Red hordes back over the 38th parallel. The city of Seoul was almost completely flattened in that war, and its rebuilding and growth in the short space of thirty-five years to become the seventh-largest city in the world, replete with thousands of flourishing churches, is a modern miracle.

It is out of the furnace of suffering that the Korean church has emerged to become such a potent force in world Christianity. The story of how the revival in Korea has been maintained in the face of persecution and poverty, and in contending with the more subtle pressures occasioned by the sudden prosperity which has come with economic growth, is a lesson for the affluent West. Can revival live with affluence? So far the Korean revival has come to terms with the nation's prosperity because they regard it as God's way of enabling them to engage in world evangelism on an unprecedented scale. The Christian world is watching with bated breath to see if the Korean church can break through the prosperity barrier to become a world missionary nation, spreading revival to the ends of the earth.

Because we were in Korea in June 1987 when the student demonstrations for more democracy and completely free elections were happening, we became vividly aware of the many problems which beset the nation, and Christians especially. Such an experience wiped away any lingering tendencies to a triumphalistic view of the Korean church and nation—there are plenty of warts on both. Each of them has come a long way in a very short time, but both have still a long, long way to go before they gain their objectives.

The staging of the Olympics in Korea in 1988 has allowed the world to focus in on this colourful and volatile nation. Whatever Christians are doing in other parts of the world, a great host of Korean Christians are going for gold, in the spiritual sense. Great characters such as Dr Jashil Choi, Yonggi Cho's mother-in-law, the amazing lady who started his Prayer Mountain where thousands go to pray and fast. And Dr Kim Sun-Do, the senior minister of the world's largest Methodist Church, Kwang Lim, Seoul, who was a medical doctor before answering God's call on his life to enter the ministry. Dr Kim, is a truly humble man of God, with a gracious spirit and possessing an aggressive urge for evangelism; a true son of authentic Methodism whom it was thrilling to meet and hear. Some two hundred and fifty years after the conversion of John Wesley, it is good to know that the torch still flames in this far-off corner of Wesley's world parish. Such people, along with a whole galaxy of others whom we met, constitute one of the great reasons behind the Korean miracle. You will meet many of them in the pages of this book.

But be warned, Korea is no Utopia, spiritually or naturally. Before you go rushing off to Korea thinking that it is paradise on earth, realise this—it is no easier to pray in Korea than in Britain or America or Australia; it is just as hard to win souls in Korea as in Africa or any place else. They have advanced on their knees, every yard of spiritual territory they have taken has had to be wrested from the enemy of souls.

In many areas Koreans are an enigma to Westerners, even to those who have spent many years in their land. On the one hand Koreans are very beautiful in their appearance. Their standard of dress is of the highest, and every day most of them seemed to be dressed as though for Sunday. Although many of their homes are very small, the ladies—old and young—always looked as though they had just stepped out of a 'band box'. The men also were immaculate: even in hot weather they nearly all wore a suit and a collar and tie. We scarcely saw one pair of jeans being worn. Would you believe, the only hippy we saw turned out to be British! We were most impressed by their dress. In fact, when we arrived back in Britain we felt ashamed and humbled as we realised that the British in everyday clothing compared most unfavourably.

On the other hand, Koreans hate to lose face and never give way if they can help it. This makes them seem very pushy and even rude on occasions. They don't believe in apologising even if they bump quite hard into you. One of the things which we found hard to bear was the constant pushing in the stores and shops. Koreans will walk into you as though you do not exist and will push past you in a taxi queue as though you are not there; banging and bumping into other shoppers seems to be simply part of everyday life which is taken for granted. They don't seem to mind knocking into you and don't see the need to apologise for it; neither do they seem to mind in the least if you barge into them during your shopping expedition, and certainly do not expect you to apologise.

Korean Christians are also an enigma in some vital areas of inter-church relationships, even in the midst of the revival. I will never forget the sadness of Dr Edwin Orr at his week's conference on revival at Oxford in the summer of 1984. He had been a guest of honour at the great Korean centenary celebrations in Seoul just a few weeks before. With much enthusiasm and expectancy I asked him about the celebrations, and especially about the united prayer gathering attended by more than a million Koreans who prayed all night on the vast Plaza. He said that it was impressive and wonderful in many ways, but as one who was a frequent visitor and therefore knew them well, he found that 'it was marred by their usual rivalries and factions'. The Korean church is no more perfect than was the church at Corinth or at Ephesus. However, I found this more of a help than a hindrance; I was encouraged to realise that God is so gracious that he will bless in the most extraordinary ways even an imperfect church—all he asks is that we believe him and allow him to work. The message of what God has done and is doing in Korea is very relevant to the church everywhere and especially in the West.

2

The Miracle of the Word

Prayer is certainly the supreme secret behind the phenomenal growth of the church in Korea, but it is not the only one. Everybody who knows anything at all about the growth immediately thinks of prayer and then most probably of house cells. They fail to realise the underlying priority that is given to the word of God, both in preaching and in studying. Without the solid foundation of the word even the most devout and fervent praying can all too easily go astray.

Yonggi Cho and the majority of Korean pastors are people of the word. From the very first, priority has been given to God's word in the many flourishing evangelical churches which abound not only in the capital city of Seoul but throughout the nation. Yonggi Cho is quick to tell you that in his ever-growing church they first seek to build faith through Bible study and teaching before joining together in group prayer. He says: 'God's word is the Truth and the Truth casts out unbelief.'

The pulpit of Yonggi Cho's Yoido Full Gospel Church is a word-centred one. Whenever he preaches, you can be sure that his message is based firmly on the Scriptures and is mainly exposition of the word of God. Whenever his associate senior ministers preach (and they regularly share the pulpit with him in this great church), you can be sure that you are going to hear the word of God expounded and the gospel preached. Yonggi Cho takes his preaching very seriously indeed. Although he has now established this world-famous church and could easily sit back and repreach some of his old messages, he does not do so, but still prepares very thoroughly before he preaches. He gives his people positive, faith-building messages. He will tell you that although he is most frequently questioned by people about his house cells, his church is not only growing by cells. He insists that one of the most important things is good preaching, giving people a good message which really meets their needs. He boldly declares: 'I believe that the word of God was written by the correct and infallible inspiration of the Holy Spirit.'

It is a tremendous thrill to see the vast crowds flocking to Yoido Full Gospel Church to hear the word of God, not only at the seven great services on Sundays (at 6.30, 9 and 11 am, 1, 3, 5 and 7 pm) but also three times on Wednesdays (at 2, 5 and 7 pm) and twice on Saturdays (at 3 and 5 pm). Furthermore, the great sanctuary is always filled. These are essentially preaching services: the message on Sundays is usually a clear gospel-type sermon lasting thirty to forty minutes, whilst on Wednesdays and Saturdays a full hour is often devoted to an expositional Bible study. There is also quite a lot of red-hot preaching during the all-night prayer meetings.

The building at Yoido was dedicated on 23rd September 1973 and at first was capable of seating ten thousand people (Korean style, that is, because Koreans generally are much smaller and slimmer than Westerners and happily cram in several more per pew than we would accept). This was extended, and when finished at the end of 1985 the main sanctuary was capable of seating 25,000. In addition, there are fifteen auxiliary chapels, all connected by close-circuit television, which almost double that figure, giving a total capacity of close on 50,000.

The eagerness with which they gather on the hottest of

days to hear the word of God is a sight for sore eyes. The readiness with which they respond to the preaching with fervent hallelujahs, amens and brief assents in Korean, indicates how avidly they listen. This seems to draw the best out of Yonggi Cho, who is an excellent preacher and a great communicator. He has a delightful sense of humour and is not afraid to tell a story against himself—and how his people love that! They laugh with him and appreciate his genuine humanity, that he is fallible just like them.

In his sermon on one of the Sunday mornings we were there he preached a message entitled 'The Humble Heart'. In the course of it he shared how on one occasion recently he had been visiting one of the city hospitals and afterwards was waiting for the lift down. Each time the lift opened it was full and could take no more. After this had happened several times he had the idea that next time the lift was going up he would get in and travel up with it to the top floor and then stay in and come down. As he stepped in, the girl in charge of the lift asked him where he was going and when she discovered that he was intending to go up only in order to travel down, she ordered him to get out again—in front of all the people in the lift as well as those who had been waiting with him outside the lift. He was humiliated and angry. He told this girl who he was but she was adamant—those were her orders, people were not allowed to get in the lift and travel up in order to get a place on it coming down. 'Out!' she said. 'Doesn't this girl know I am the pastor of a big church?' he said to himself. He blustered and protested but all in vain. This slip of a girl did not care who he was or how much he protested, 'Get out!' she shouted. There was nothing for it but to obey, which he did with bad grace.

The packed auditorium rocked with laughter as he described that such was his indignation that when she turned her back on him he clenched his fist behind her!

They identified with him so readily in this everyday situation. The one thing Koreans hate to do is to lose face in front of others. Their nature and culture abhor having to back down or give way. The thought of a lift girl getting the better of their senior pastor was something to savour. Then he shared how afterwards at home when he had cooled down and was praying about it, the Holy Spirit began to speak to him and remind him that this girl was just as important in God's sight as he was. She was every bit as precious to God and was only doing her job and carrying out her orders. He repented and humbled himself before God.

The rest of the sermon was taken up with explaining how God had had to humble such great Bible characters as Joseph, Abraham, Jacob and Moses. God had to humble every one of them before he could use them. He climaxed it by revealing how the Lord Jesus was the perfect example of the humble heart who always did the Father's will perfectly—even to the cross.

It was superb Bible preaching. Behind it lay much prayer and preparation. Yonggi Cho says that getting his message from God and preparing it for the people is his number one priority. His method of working is interesting. He rests on Mondays, and who can blame him? He puts so much into his preaching that at the end of a Sunday he feels utterly drained, and more than once he has told his wife that he feels empty and has nothing left to preach. By Tuesday, however, he is praying and seeking the Lord for next Sunday's message. On Thursday he must be ready to give the subject of his sermon so that the title of it can be printed in the weekly bulletin. (When you are printing hundreds of thousands of them you cannot put it off until Friday!) Friday night he does not go home at all but remains in the church and spends all night praying and writing out his message. He has said, 'When I was a greenbean, I thought it was very easy to preach, but now every word that proceeds out of my mouth is being

watched by the government and the Christian world, by
my friends and by my enemies.' When he stands to preach
he feels sure that God has given him not just a message
but the message for the people on that day and for that
time—that is the kind of *rhema* (word) which I am certain
no one would quarrel about.

Before I went to Korea I thought that with such
numbers I was bound to find people who were rather
'frothy' and not very well taught. To use an 'in' word, I
was not very optimistic about finding them discipled. I
was delighted to discover my fears were groundless. The
believers in Korea are generally much better taught than
their counterparts in Britain. Not only is the preaching
word-centred, but the teaching in the house cells is word-
centred as well. Nothing is left to chance. House cell
leaders are trained before being put in charge, but then
every week they are issued with the teaching notes for
their group. It is an amazing sight to see them unloading
a whole lorry load of over half a million teaching leaflets
every Saturday afternoon, ready for distribution on
Sunday. In addition, at Yoido Full Gospel Church they
prepare a Bible textbook for the cell leaders every six
months. Nothing is left to chance.

But Yonggi Cho will say that his church (apart from
being the biggest) is not unique. All the churches which
are sound in the faith (and most of them are) are growing
at a tremendous rate. For a Britisher it is an unbelievable
experience to go straight from one of the packed services
at Yoido Full Gospel Church a little way across the city
to the Kwang Lim Methodist Church and find Dr Kim
Sun-Do preaching to his fourth congregation of the day,
several thousand strong. True, he has a congregation of
a mere forty thousand or so, and therefore can manage
with only four services on a Sunday instead of Cho's
seven. But here again the word is central, both in the
main services and in the thousands of house cells.

If you have any unbelieving breath still left in you, then

a quick trip to another part of the city to the famous Young Nak Presbyterian Church will surely expel that very quickly. To see the thousands streaming in and out of this, the largest Presbyterian church in the world, is a great faith booster. Though there are some very real differences doctrinally between this and Cho's church, there are many similarities — principally their word-centredness, faithful Bible preaching, house cells and regular all-nights of prayer.

All the great church leaders in Korea today acknowledge their abiding debt to the first Protestant missionaries, who in the main were all orthodox in their faith and resolute believers of the word of God. Although the first Roman Catholic missionary arrived in Korea in 1794, almost a century before the Protestants, the Protestant Church soon outstripped the Catholic Church and vastly outnumbers it today. The early Catholic missionaries and their converts certainly did not lack courage, since they proved themselves willing to suffer hardship and imprisonment. Not only that but tens of thousands of them became martyrs for the cause, proving faithful unto death. But their great weakness was their failure to teach and translate the Scriptures, whereas the Protestants sought from the very beginning to distribute Bibles, and gave top priority to translating the Scriptures into the Korean language.

The first Protestant martyr was a Welshman, Robert Jermain Thomas, who was ordained at Hanover Chapel, Abergavenny, in 1863. That same year he and his wife left for China under the auspices of the London Missionary Society. The climate proved too hot for his wife and within a short time she died, leaving Thomas broken-hearted. He moved to Chefoo in 1865, and became interested in the mysterious land of Korea through the arrival of two Korean Catholics who had risked their lives by hiding on board a junk from Korea bound for China. Alexander Williamson was the agent for the National Bible Society of Scotland stationed in Chefoo, and was appalled to discover how ignorant these two Korean Catholics were of the Scriptures. Robert Thomas volunteered to return to the forbidden land of Korea with these two brave men, and offered to act as agent for the Bible Society on the trip. They sailed on a junk from Chefoo on 4th September 1865, and arrived at the Korean coast on the 13th. Thomas spent some two-and-a-half months exploring the territory, and as well as acquiring something of the language he also distributed a good number of Chinese Bibles. Those who received them did so at the risk of being decapitated, it being a capital offence to have a Bible. Thomas sailed from Korea to Manchuria in December and then travelled overland, eventually arriving in Peking in January 1866.

Furious persecution broke out against the Catholics in Korea in 1866 and things were in a real ferment. A French admiral was preparing an expedition to Korea to demand redress for the killing of some French priests, and he asked Robert Thomas to accompany him as one who knew a little bit about the country. However, there was a delay and Thomas embarked on an American ship instead. This one was called *General Sherman*, and was loaded with goods with a view to opening trading with Korea. Its intentions seemed honourable and Thomas boarded the vessel with a good supply of Bibles and New Testaments in Chinese. Subsequent inquiries by another ship's captain after the tragic destruction of the *General Sherman* revealed otherwise, and it would seem that, as well as being loaded with guns and explosives and contraband goods, the ship's company had ideas about plundering the royal tombs in Pyongyang. Thomas was oblivious to any of this, and his motives were certainly above question.

The *General Sherman* entered the mouth of the Taitong river towards the end of August 1866. The Korean governor of the province sent an urgent message asking why they had come. They replied that they wished to

begin trading with Korea. This was apparently the last
thing the governor wanted and he was definitely scared
at the prospect. Korea as a whole at this time was still
vainly trying to shut herself off from the rest of the world
in an attempt to preserve her traditions. In spite of what
the governor said the ship proceeded up the river, which
was flooded due to heavy rain. This factor, coupled with
a high tide, enabled them to pass the bar below the city
of Pyongyang. However, as soon as the tide receded, the
ship was left stranded in the mud.

On their way up the river, at Kang-so-po-san, Robert
Thomas took the opportunity to throw some Chinese New
Testaments to some of the Koreans standing on the shore.
Years later, a Korean who was being instructed in the
faith and who was received into the church by a Dr
Moffett, said that his father had received one of these New
Testaments.

At Suk-som the commander of the Korean garrison
came aboard demanding assurances from them; unwisely,
the captain attempted to hold hostage the commander
and three of his escorts. They eventually escaped, aided
by a young man called Pak Chu-Kwom, who later became
one of the first Christians in the city.

The situation was now very dangerous and the ship
opened fire, causing casualties and further inflaming
matters. The ship being now firmly stuck in the mud,
they continued firing intermittently for about two weeks.
The crew became desperate and sued for peace, apologising to the governor, who told them all to appear before
him. They were suspicious that it was a trap, refused
and opened fire again. Understandably the Koreans were
provoked to retaliate. They prepared a large flat-bottomed
boat filled with brushwood and sulphur, and it was set
on fire and allowed to drift down the river alongside the
General Sherman, which was a wooden vessel. All too soon
the ship caught fire and the crew panicked and dived
overboard into the water. They were all killed as they

came ashore. Robert Thomas took some of his Bibles with him and managed to reach land safely. He offered a Bible to one of the Koreans who found him, but it was refused. He realised his danger and knelt down and prayed before the man killed him. Somehow the Korean got the impression that Thomas was a good man and decided to take the book home with him. Very wonderfully, years later this man's nephew, Lee Young-Tai, worked with Dr W D Reynolds on revision of the early Bible translation.

Also in the crowd watching the burning ship was a young boy who received three of the Bibles given out by Thomas. Afraid to keep them himself he passed them on to a soldier, who took them home and used the pages to paper his house. Years later when the boy became a Christian, he visited that house and saw the Bible pages pasted on the wall.

News of the brave Robert Thomas's martyrdom stirred many Christians to pray, and the Bible Societies were determined to get the Bible into the hands of Koreans in whatever way possible. The first missionary to get involved in translating the Scriptures into the Korean language was a Scottish Presbyterian missionary working in Manchuria, the Revd John Ross. He found a Korean willing to serve him as a language teacher and in due course he began the arduous task of translating the Scriptures. Ross eventually completed the translation of Luke's Gospel and the National Bible Society of Scotland got it printed. It was published in 1881. Within three years and with the help of the British and Foreign Bible Society, they published Ross's translation of all four Gospels and Acts.

In very many ways John Ross was the real Protestant pioneer in Christian work among Koreans; unable to work inside the country he worked just over the border in Manchuria, contacting Koreans who had settled there or who were travelling through. Chinese Bibles and Korean Gospels were smuggled in, at great personal risk to the

brave souls who volunteered for the task. Ross's patience
and persistence eventually paid off. The first Protestant
missionaries managed to enter Korea in 1884, and by 1887
a New Testament in Korean was ready to be published by
the British and Foreign Bible Society. Ross and his early
helpers had done an excellent job in the circumstances,
but as soon as it was feasible the Bible Societies unitedly
set out to improve the translation, working with new
Korean Christian scholars. In 1900 this much better
version was dedicated at a great thanksgiving service in
Chung Dong Methodist Church.

From the first, the sale of Korean Bibles really took off.
The pioneer missionaries wisely stressed the importance
of converts learning their Bibles, and did everything possible to ensure that all had their own copies. It is one of
the abiding factors in the strong growth of the Korean
church. Another factor was the use of the Korean alphabet
known as the hangul. Koreans are a separate race with a
distinct language which is neither Chinese nor Japanese;
but until the invention of the simplified hangul alphabet
by their great King Seijong in 1450, the written language
was virtually the prerogative of the learned scholars—
and it suited them to keep it that way.

It was claimed that King Seijong's system was so
ingeniously simple that even a woman could learn it!
After the scholars had spent many years mastering the
complicated Chinese classics, they were certainly not
going to let everyone get hold of the key of knowledge
because reading had been made simple. Thus until the
Bible was translated into it, the hangul script was largely
ignored and used only for the lowest type of novels. It
was as though the loving kiss of the faithful Bible translators had at last awakened this sleeping beauty of a
phonetic writing system. The literacy rate among new
Christians climbed rapidly, as they were so eager to read
the word of God for themselves. It quickly affected Korean
society as a whole, and today Korea stands as one of the

most literate nations in the world with a claimed 92 per cent literacy, which places them higher then even Britain or America. Who can deny that the wisdom of God was wonderfully at work through those first faithful Bible translators in Korea?

3

The Miracle of Continuing Revival

The first time I heard Yonggi Cho preach was at Minehead, England, in 1981. By that time his church had
already passed the 150,000 mark, and he told us that by
the end of the year he was confident they would burst
through the 200,000 barrier. His immediate faith-goal was
a quarter of a million, but after much prayer he felt that
God had given him the faith to believe for half a million
members. Sitting there on the platform I was frankly
totally unbelieving. I thought this dapper and charming
little Oriental had really gone beyond all bounds of possi-
bility. My mind just could not take it in. The figure
was more than the total membership of any British Free
Church denomination. Sitting there I felt rather sorry for
him; on this occasion he clearly had blundered badly.

Early in 1986 I was soon reading that just before the
end of 1985 his church had attained the magic figure of
half a million members. And in 1987 when Kingsway
Publications asked me to write this book, I was privileged
to go and see for myself. I feel a close sense of kinship
with Abraham's wife, Sarah, when the Lord caught her
laughing in unbelief behind the tent flap at the
preposterous notion of her becoming a mother at ninety
years of age (Gen 18:10–15). After sitting there on the
platform at Minehead in front of several thousand people,
inwardly smirking at this little Korean preacher's ridicu-

lous notion of a church of half a million members, here I am writing about it after seeing it for myself and investigating it in depth. Who says the Lord has not got a sense of humour?

However, when I got to Korea I found that the Lord had by no means completed my education. Looking at the vast congregation and learning something of the tremendous travail that lay behind this staggering venture of faith, I found myself with deep sympathy for another wife—Mrs Yonggi Cho. I could understand her asking him to stop at half a million members. This he more or less promised her he would do since the pressures involved in this kind of growth are overwhelming. But when he was with his wife in Japan, not so very long ago, as they were praying and praising God together during their devotional time in the hotel, God spoke into his heart once again and gave him a vision of enlarging his church for a further 200,000 by 1990: in other words, a grand total of 700,000 members. He shook his head, afraid to tell his wife. But she knows him only too well after all these years and she quickly sensed what had happened. With the typical fortitude of a faithful and loving wife she accepted it. She also knows that he is unlikely to stop at 700,000 members, and if God spares him he will inevitably go on to a million. Already they are preparing satellite chapels around the city to be linked by close-circuit television to the central building.

There are over 25,000 Protestant congregations in South Korea. Apart from the three mega-churches in Seoul which we have mentioned already, there are others numbering 10,000, and congregations of over 1,000 are common. Together these total around ten million believers; add to that about one-and-a-half million Roman Catholics and already the nation is effectively over 25 per cent Christian. With spiritual new births taking place at around one million per year as against the natural births at about 600,000 per year, the goal of being more than

50 per cent Christian by the early 1990s and then going on to take the nation seems clearly attainable. (Not that they have any idea of stopping when they have taken the nation! The goal of the whole Korean church seems to be of becoming a nation wholly committed to God which he can take hold of for world evangelism.) If you take into account the fact that Seoul and whole areas of South Korea were almost wiped out during the 1950–3 Korean War, you begin to have some idea of the miracle behind such figures.

If the idea of Korea as a nation being used in a special way seems fantastic and unrealistic, I for one have learned not to rule anything out where these people are concerned. When the young D L Moody heard a preacher say: 'The world has yet to see what God can do with and through a man wholly consecrated to Him,' he responded in his heart, 'By the grace of God, I will be that man.' And it is now a matter of history just how wonderfully God did use him. I wonder, is the world about to see what God can do with a nation that is wholly yielded to him? In the story of the continuing revival in Korea we are being allowed to witness history in the making. It commenced eighty years ago when the missionaries and the early believers prayed through until the fire fell. It is an object lesson for the church in the West which has grown soft through years of apathy and affluence.

The year of 1907 is indelibly burned into the story of the Korean church, just as 1904 is forever written in letters of fire in that of the Welsh church. The revival of 1907 marked the great turning-point when the Holy Spirit moved in power and the church made the all-important transition from being a foreign missionary enterprise to having a truly Korean identity. Korean Christians still look back to 1907 as a mighty move of the Holy Spirit which marks the source of their spiritual life.

The pioneer Presbyterian and Methodist missionaries, from the time of their entry into the country in 1884, had done a marvellous job in the crucial years leading up to 1907. For the most part the missionaries were of the Puritan type, holding aloof from things which they regarded as worldly blights such as dancing, smoking, gambling, drinking and the like. Theologically they were conservative, holding firmly that the Scriptures were inspired, and believing fervently the premillennial teaching of the Second Coming of Christ. They laid a solid foundation, aiming for true conversions with a new-birth experience. They were also sufficiently enlightened to adopt indigenous principles from the very beginning. As early as June 1890, the pioneer Presbyterian missionary Dr Underwood invited the experienced Revd John Nevius over from China to discuss missionary principles. In the main they adopted what have now become known as 'the Nevius Methods', namely self-support, self-government and self-propagation of indigenous churches. They concentrated on teaching the Bible and fostering local leadership. Koreans were given responsibilities and allowed to share in shaping their church in every way possible. They played a vital part, along with the missionaries, in translating the Scriptures, which helped to give these something of a Korean idiom.

In the early days a new convert who wanted to be baptised had to have led another person to Christ. Standards were kept high. Before an illiterate person was allowed to receive Communion they had to learn to read. Even old people had to learn to read the Bible before they could be baptised. Tithing was obligatory for all believers. Those first Korean Christians were well and truly discipled. Samuel A Moffett came to Korea in 1890 and in 1903 was the founding president of the Presbyterian Seminary in Pyongyang. Towards the end of his presidency he could say: 'I have done what I prayed and decided before God when I came to Korea. That is, I decided not to preach anything except the cross of Christ. If I preach any other gospel, I should be cursed.'

As soon as the missionaries were given freedom to preach they found a growing response to the gospel, especially in the north of the country around the large town of Pyongyang, which had a population of some 60,000 in 1894. That was the year in which the Sino-Japanese war broke out, and the town was nearly destroyed in the fierce fighting between the Chinese and the Japanese. Finally the Japanese succeeded in driving out the Chinese soldiers, but the population of the town was reduced to 15,000 and the small group of new Christians were scattered around the province, witnessing to their new-found faith everywhere they went. Samuel Moffett reported that the war had 'shaken the whole nation of Korea from its lethargy and extreme conservatism'. The infant church had been built on a good foundation and was ready to take advantage of the situation. There were just fifty-two members in the Pyongyang church in 1894 and Moffett bravely returned from the safer area of Seoul to care for them during the days of the fighting. He was a true pastor and his courage and love for the little flock did not go unnoticed. The decade following 1894 was one of rapid growth. By 1896 the membership in the churches had trebled. It grew from 73 in 1895 to 1,058 in 1898 (these were communicants—the number of adherents was double that, giving a total of at least 3,000).

The wonderful thing was that it was the Koreans themselves who were largely responsible for the spread of the gospel. As soon as people were converted they could not keep it to themselves, they felt impelled to tell their relatives and friends. Again and again these zealous new converts found their relatives open to the gospel and a new group of believers was planted. The missionaries could not keep up with the new congregations that were being planted all over the province, let alone the numbers of new believers. They wisely concentrated on teaching these groups of new believers and on training the leadership which was emerging. Many of the converts were heads of families, and such was the structure of Korean society that the rest of the family followed almost as a matter of course.

A new congregation was started in 1896 in an insignificant little town called Sunchun in the northern part of the province. Out of a population of only 3,000 there was soon a congregation of 500. When the Japanese decided to build the Pusan to Manchuria railway in 1905, they elected to put it right through Sunchun, which thus became an important centre of communication. The church became a boomtown one and other new groups soon sprang up around it. There was a bigger response to the gospel in the north at this time than in the city of Seoul and other areas in the south.

The first stirrings of revival occurred in 1903. With so many flocking in to the fledgling churches, the missionaries realised the necessity of teaching and training the converts if the church was to be kept holy in life and sound in doctrine. In August 1903 a group of Methodist missionaries met together in Wonsan, under the leadership of a missionary from China, Miss M C White. A Canadian medical missionary, Dr R A Hardie, was also a member of the group. He had gone to Korea in 1890 with the Canadian Colleges' Mission, but in 1898 he transferred to the Southern Methodist Mission and engaged in evangelistic work in Wonsan. He was in charge of a pioneer work in Kangwon province, but the work was difficult and progress was so slow that he felt himself a failure. All his self-sufficiency was broken down and he was brought to the end of himself. During the conference he humbled himself before God and his missionary colleagues, openly confessing his pride, hardness of heart and lack of faith. He had yearned to see Koreans convicted of sin and brought into a real experience of new birth, but first God had to deal with him. After confessing his own deep need, he was in a position to claim by simple faith the gift of the Holy Spirit. Filled with the Spirit, the renewed Dr Hardie humbled himself still further by confessing his failure before the Korean church. As a result, many of the Koreans understood for the first time what conviction and repentance really meant, and some of them confessed their shortcomings also. It was a beginning.

Dr Hardie was soon preparing for the visit of the missionary advocate Fredrik Franson in October 1903. During Franson's week of meetings confession of sins was again a special feature, with many confessing to thefts and making restitution. Franson also taught Hardie and his colleagues the secret of prevailing prayer. He would cry, 'O Father, Thou canst do it; Thou wilt do it; Thou shalt do it.' The church was cleansed and renewed in this first wave of revival.

The week's Bible conference at Wonsan was repeated the following year with similar results and even greater blessing. Up to this point it was very much a local renewal, but as news filtered through of what God was doing at these Bible and prayer conference weeks at Wonsan, similar gatherings were organised in other areas.

1905 was a crisis year in the nation, when the Japanese finally defeated Russia and took control of Korea as the spoils of war. Many urged the churches to lead the nation in organised resistance against the Japanese, but the missionaries and church leaders wisely refused to get involved in political action and concentrated on preaching the gospel. There was a real danger of a general uprising, which the missionaries knew had no chance of success and could only result in further humiliation and bloodshed. Those were anxious days, and further stimulated the missionaries to seek God earnestly in prayer. They were encouraged by the increasing number of conversions almost everywhere as the second wave of revival rolled in.

In 1906 the missionaries at Pyongyang planned a Bible

conference in August and invited Dr Hardie to address them. He was still enjoying the personal revival he had experienced in 1903, and his ministry was much blessed as they studied the First Epistle of John, which subsequently became the textbook during the revival. In the autumn the Revd Howard Agnew Johnson of New York came to Korea and fanned the flames as he told them of the great revival in Wales in 1904–5, and how it had spread to the Welsh Presbyterian missionaries in India. Following his visit a noon prayer meeting was commenced and this continued daily for many months, leading up to the third wave of full revival.

The revival wave finally broke upon the Men's Annual Bible Conference week in the Central Church in Pyongyang in January 1907. On the Saturday evening of 6th January there were 1,500 men packed in the building. The Revd W N Blair preached a powerful message on 1 Corinthians 12:27, 'Now ye are the body of Christ, and members in particular,' in which he showed that discord in the church was like sickness in our bodies. Many were brought under conviction and confessed their lack of love for other believers.

Sunday, the 7th, was something of a disappointment: the meetings were crowded but the missionaries were conscious of real spiritual opposition blocking the blessing, causing a feeling of deadness. They felt as exhausted and drained by the end of the day as if they had been engaged in actual physical conflict. Next morning the missionaries met for prayer and called on God in great earnestness. That night the atmosphere was entirely different. The presence of God filled the place. There was a short sermon and then the Revd Graham Lee took over and asked for prayers. The response was immediate; many men were suddenly on their feet praying aloud, simultaneously. Graham Lee had the spiritual wisdom to discern that God was in this and he said,

'If you want to pray like that, all pray.' Eye-witnesses

said the result was indescribable, as the whole congregation of 1,500 men lifted their voices in prayer to Almighty God. It was like the sound of many waters, a veritable Niagara, 'the surf of an ocean of prayer beating against God's throne. It was not many but one, born of one Spirit.' This new phenomenon of united, audible prayer continued throughout the revival, and to this very day remains a remarkable feature of Korean Christianity.

The reality of this praying was soon evident when an intense conviction of sin settled on the meeting, and before long many were weeping bitterly and confessing their sins. Graham Lee described what he saw:

> Man after man would rise, confess his sin, break down and weep, and then throw himself on the floor and beat the floor in a perfect agony of conviction. Sometimes after a confession, the whole audience would break out into audible prayer, and the effect of hundreds of men praying together was indescribable. Again, after another confession, they would break out into uncontrollable weeping and we would all weep together. We couldn't help it. And so the meeting went on until 2 am with confession and weeping and praying. (From a pamphlet by William N Blair *The Korea Pentecost*, quoted in *History of Protestant Missions in Korea*.)

The next night, Tuesday, was even more remarkable. Two elders had long been at loggerheads with each other, and in the meeting after a fierce inner struggle one of the elders made his way to the pulpit and confessed that he had been guilty of fighting against God. He acknowledged that he was guilty of hating not only his brother elder but the missionary (the Revd W M Blair) as well. He turned to Blair and asked for his forgiveness and for his prayers. Blair only got as far as praying, 'Father, Father!' when the Spirit of God descended upon them like an avalanche of power. The effect was immediate, overwhelming and terrifying. Some threw themselves full length on the floor, while others stood with their arms raised to heaven; all were pleading with God for mercy. The missionaries were afraid of what was happening but dared not interfere, knowing that this was the work of the Holy Spirit and the very thing they had prayed for. Eventually, Graham Lee was able to start a hymn, and then followed the most awful confessions of sin which hundreds of men seemed compelled to make in an attempt to relieve their souls of the agony of conviction under which the Holy Spirit had brought them. Proud men were humbled and broken as the awesome holiness of God overwhelmed them. Others were so troubled by their consciences that they were dumb and could only clench their fists and strike their heads against the ground in a vain effort to find relief as the Spirit of God dealt with them.

When the meetings ended, the men returned to their homes around the region on fire for God, burning with an unquenchable zeal. Everywhere they went the revival spread with the same remarkable manifestations of deep conviction of sin, weeping and brokenness, public confession of sins followed by restitution wherever possible, and the settling of quarrels by forgiveness. The whole of the city of Pyongyang was stirred and affected as men went from house to house, confessing to those they had wronged, returning stolen property and money to both Christians and non-Christians. A Chinese merchant could hardly believe it when a Christian walked into his shop and paid him a large sum of money he had obtained by wrong means years before.

With the same results the revival swept through the colleges of both men and women, leaving students permanently changed for the better. Even the schools had to suspend lessons as the children came under the mighty influence of the Holy Spirit, leading them to weep and confess their wrongdoings. What happened in 1907 far surpassed all that had gone beforehand. This was a nation-wide revival. Dr Hardie and his missionary colleagues spread the revival in every place they visited, and Korean leaders such as the Revd Kil Sun-Joo of Pyongyang soon became household names as they convened revival meetings across the nation. The same revival phenomena ocurred everywhere, but it was noted that the power of the move in each place could almost be determined by the extent of the public confession of sins and the fervour of the prayer in unison of those assembled. This move of the Holy Spirit permanently affected the Korean church: it established its own special Korean character. Its spiritual worth was tested to the hilt in the years of fierce persecution which followed under Japanese occupation, but the revival was divine preparation for the trial.

A year after the revival, a Methodist missionary bishop, M C Harris, gave his considered assessment that,

> the effects following this movement are wholly good; the church has been raised to a higher spiritual level. Scores have been called to the ministry; larger congregations are searching the word. Drunkards, gamblers, thieves, adulterers, murderers, self-righteous Confucians, and dead Buddhists, and thousands of devil-worshippers have been made new men in Christ, the old things gone forever. (From The Journal of the 25th Delegated General Conference of the Methodist Church in 1908, pp 861–862.)

No less a person than Lord William Cecil wrote in *The Times* in glowing terms of the revival, likening it to the Wesleyan revival:

> The Koreans who were at the original meetings have gone forth, like Wesley's converts, their preaching has been wonderfully successful—so much so that there are not a few who say that it is through Korea that the light of Christianity will shine to the Far Eastern world.

When one considers that those words were written in May 1908, one appreciates the accuracy of their prophetic insight when viewing the Korean church today.

4

The Miracle of a Praying People

The praying of the Korean church is unique in the twentieth century. While the prayer life of the churches in the West has declined, in Korea it has not only been sustained throughout the century but has actually increased. The sudden emergence of the feature of thousands praying aloud simultaneously, which marked the revival of 1907, is a mark of the continuing revival. That is one form of intercession which can be witnessed regularly in thousands of churches in Korea today. But it is not the only kind of praying they do; the secret of the Korean church is that they practise every kind. It is surely what Paul is talking about when he refers to 'praying always with all prayer and supplication in the Spirit, and watching thereunto with all perseverance and supplication for all saints' (Eph 6:18). In the West we believe in prayer; in Korea they believe in praying! There the level of praying is inspiring. They all pray, they are always doing so, and they intercede in every way possible. They pray alone and in twos; they pray in small groups and in their homes; they pray in their churches and on their mountains; they pray in their own language and they pray 'in the Spirit' in other tongues; they pray silently and loudly (sometimes very loudly); they pray with tears and with holy laughter; they sing their prayers and sometimes they groan their prayers as they intercede and get under burdens which the Holy Spirit lays upon them; they pray in the morning and in the evening; they pray at midday and at midnight; they pray with fasting and they pray over their meals; they pray for their friends and for their enemies; they pray for their neighbour and for their nation; they pray for the church and for the world; they pray for everyone and about everything.

In the West we flit from one kind of praying to another according to the latest fad. One minute the only way to pray is in small groups of three or four, and the old-type prayer meeting is denigrated as boring. Next, the only way to pray is to meditate and the small groups are out of fashion. In Korea they know that the only way to sustain their God-given revival is by all kinds of praying by all Christians all the time.

Yonggi Cho is emphatic that for revival you have to organise massive prayer if you are ever to experience a great outpouring of the Holy Spirit. This is something which is sadly missing in Western churches today, though some brave souls are seeking to remedy this. We have become so used to the prayer meeting being the smallest meeting that we have grown to accept it as a fact of spiritual life in the 1980s. It is, therefore, a tremendous tonic to visit Korea, where prayer meetings are not meas- ured in handfuls of mainly women and elderly people but in thousands of men and women and vast numbers of young people; and the frequency and duration of the prayer meeting is daily and for many hours instead of just weekly and for a few minutes.

It is a Western pastor's dream come true to find people queuing to get into an all-night prayer meeting and to see them struggling to find a seat in a beautiful, circular auditorium, much larger and more modern than London's Royal Albert Hall. Such is the experience every Friday night in the Yoido Full Gospel Church. It is not a case of whipping up support for some special effort, it is the normal, weekly, all-night Friday prayer meeting lasting from 10 pm until 5 a.m. The ones who usually leave around midnight are the few dozen visitors from the West who find themselves in Seoul for one reason or another; the ones who stay right through are the Koreans.

The Friday all-night prayer service in Yonggi Cho's church at Yoido is superbly organised, along with everything else in this mega-church of over half a million members; which it obviously needs to be if utter confusion is to be avoided. As foreigners, my wife Hazel and I were quickly spotted even in the great sea of jet-black Korean heads, and were greeted by a special steward wearing a beautiful satin sash inscribed: 'Welcome Foreigners'. In passable English he welcomed us and then asked us to follow him as he showed us up to the special section set aside in the gallery for foreign visitors. All the pews in this section are fitted with headphones, and a regular team working on a rota translate the main services on Sunday, Wednesday, Friday and Saturday. This is quite a task, as far fewer Koreans are fluent in English than we had imagined. We were both furnished with a hymnbook containing an excellent selection of traditional hymns in both Korean and English. The tunes were nearly all our familiar Western ones, and so we were able to join our English voices along with those of the 25,000 Koreans all around us and below us in the main body of the auditorium.

The first part of the prayer night follows a pattern not very different from other services. In fact, it is a surprise to find how very structured all the services are, and also how the order of service is almost identical in the Pentecostal, Presbyterian, Baptist and Methodist churches. In every service in the main city churches in Seoul they open with an anthem exquisitely rendered by a beautifully robed choir, accompanied by an orchestra and four-manual organ. The quality of all their church music is superb. The congregation sing a well-known gospel hymn with great enthusiasm and at a good tempo, sustained and heightened by everyone clapping in time. They never miss reciting the Apostle's Creed and do so with a conviction and clarity that would make evangelical Anglicans green with envy. You are not left in any doubt that they believe every word of it. One of the senior ministers reads a Scripture passage, followed carefully by the whole congregation from their own Bibles. The loving way they handle these and the speed with which they find the place is a clear indication that they know and love the word of God.

A senior minister leads in prayer, and every petition he utters is punctuated by fervent amens or suitable responses from the whole congregation. There are no spectators in these gatherings. Prayer is doing business with the Almighty. Over 20,000 Korean throats pour forth a torrent of assent; with one accord they back up every request made.

'Lord, bless our senior pastor, Dr Paul Yonggi Cho, and anoint your servant with the power of the Holy Spirit continually.' (Amens thunder heavenward like a mass salvo of naval guns.) 'And bless all our 487 ministers' ('Amen'), 'and every one of the 527,361 members of this church' ('Amen'). 'O Lord, bless the forty-four million people in South Korea and save all those who do not yet know you as Saviour' ('Amen! Amen!). 'And bless the twenty million people in North Korea and open the way for them to know you and for our nation to be united again' ('Amen'). 'O God, our Father, bless the outreach to Japan and you know that we are believing for the salvation of ten million Japanese by the end of this century' ('Amen! Amen! Amen!') . . .

More singing follows, either by the choir or by a smaller group of eight very talented and dedicated young people. The impression always comes through that they are singing firstly to the Lord. There is a spirit of worship and deep adoration that is apparent from their rapt expressions. Another hymn, then the offering, and the receiving of the offering is done so efficiently that it takes only a few minutes. The deacons and deaconesses (in colourful Korean dress) line up with the loaded offering bags and then march proudly down the centre aisle to the front of the great platform, where one of the senior deacons receives the bags, offers thanks for the gifts and dedicates them to the Lord for his work. It is all most impressive.

A sermon is delivered either by Yonggi Cho, if he is at home (on average he is away six months out of every year), or by one of the twenty-two senior ministers who regularly share the ministry with him. Another hymn, the singing of the Lord's Prayer, and then the serious business of prayer really begins. The senior minister officiating shares various areas of need and concern about which they should pray. As the nation is experiencing serious problems over the student demonstrations (June 1987), this is very much an urgent priority. Yonggi Cho has made it very clear to the church just what he expects of them. He does not want them to get involved in the demonstrations. At the same time he leaves them in no doubt that there is need for change in the government policy. If the nation is to prosper then increasing democratisation is urgently called for, and there must be free elections. Politicians are not in office to serve themselves or look after their own interests, but to serve the people and look after their welfare. Prayer is the greatest weapon and that is what he expects them to do, night and day, especially during the emergency.

When the senior minister indicates that he wants them all to engage in prayer for the next fifteen minutes or so on these topics, immediately the whole vast gathering starts praying. The torrent of noise is awesomely overwhelming. Not only are voices raised but hands as well. Koreans pray with all their being; many sway to and fro as they pray; others make a chopping motion with both arms together and with fists clenched—there is a holy violence about their intercession! These people are intense as they call upon God to intervene in the affairs of their beloved nation at this critical time. Many of them are old enough to remember the Korean War and the treacherous invasion by communist North Korea in June 1950. Not a few in this vast throng sampled life under the communists in North Korea before escaping to South Korea in 1953. They saw their churches closed by the communists, and many of their pastors and leaders imprisoned, tortured, and not a few martyred for their faith. These people value their freedom and their faith because they have suffered for it. Their Christian faith is their most precious possession, and they know from experience that prayer is the only real weapon against evil and oppression. That is why they pray with such fervour and passion.

Wave upon wave of praying voices rise and fall in a mighty cacophony of sound that moves one to the depths of one's soul and brings tears to the eyes. It is an experience that can never be forgotten, and leaves one shamed and humbled when it is compared with even our greatest gatherings for prayer in the West. For all the volume of sound everything is orderly. The senior minister moves to the pulpit and 'pings' a small bell of the type that used to be common in many day schools in Britain, which work by striking the button on top of a little dome. It is amplified through the amazingly efficient loudspeaker system, but even so it is not a loud noise, just a clear ping. However, it is sufficient to bring all 25,000 of them to immediate quiet. It is almost uncanny. The senior minister continues to feed in more areas needing prayer and the pattern goes on through the night. There are intervals when a striking testimony may be shared about some healing or an outstanding miracle; or further exhortations from the word may be given, inspiring faith and instructing these eager prayer warriors how to pull down the strongholds of the powers of darkness.

At five in the morning this army floods out of the great building to disperse throughout the city to their homes or jobs. Friday is the great all-night prayer gathering but Wednesday is not far behind it, and even the smaller prayer meetings on the other nights will see 2,000 packed into the Paul chapel under the main sanctuary. These different nights of prayer are taken in turns by the twenty-two districts into which the work is divided for organisational purposes. The district leaders lead the gatherings with other full-time ministers on their staff, and they organise the transport in for their members. According to my inquiries it seems that, on average, members of the church will attend one all-night of prayer per month. In addition, there are prayer meetings taking place regularly in the vast complex of rooms in the centre, and in the thousands of cells in homes and around the city in offices and factories, not to mention the thousands who make regular pilgrimages to Prayer Mountain.

Observe these people and you soon find that for them prayer is a spontaneous spiritual exercise as well as a highly organised affair. When the stewards who are on duty on Sunday gather outside the main entrance at 6 am to be briefed as to their role for the day, they form a great circle and pray. On weekday mornings hundreds of deaconesses are always coming and going from the district offices situated in the basement of the main sanctuary. If they stop and greet a particular friend, it is common to see them praying for each other before they part. Join one of the subdistrict leaders and his helpers in their car as they set off on their daily programme of visitation, and prayer is offered as a matter of course, for blessing on the ones they will meet and also for God's protection on the roads. (After a few journeys on the crowded roads in Seoul at rush hour you most certainly appreciate the need for that prayer!)

With Korea experiencing a tremendous industrial revolution in the last thirty years, the nights of prayer have tended to displace the once-familiar early morning prayer meetings of around 4.30 am, especially in the cities, although they are still quite common in rural areas. However, individual Christians in the cities religiously observe their own 'morning watch'. Although the majority of their homes are small and crowded and privacy is at a premium, they do not make that an excuse. They have learned to shut themselves in with God in a corner of their home while the rest of the household carries on around them.

All the ministers know that they are expected to begin every day with at least half an hour of private prayer, and an hour is the norm. Such dedication to prayer is costly, and Koreans get just as tired as Westerners. The people expect their pastors to lead by example when it comes to prayer. From the days when his church was smaller and they had a regular daily early morning prayer meeting, Yonggi Cho is not ashamed to relate a story or two against himself. He readily acknowledges that he complained many times about having to get up for the 4.30 am prayer meeting. Many times he had to fight extreme weariness to get there, knowing that if he was missing the people would think he was backslidden! On one occasion he did oversleep, and at 5 am his telephone rang. It was his mother-in-law, Dr Jashil Choi, demanding of him: 'Where are you? What are you doing?' (And when once you have met his mother-in-law you appreciate the story even more. She is a wonderful woman and a great prayer warrior, but not a person to be taken lightly at any time.) Pastor Yonggi Cho told her he was still in bed and wanted to know what the problem was. She soon told him. The problem was the time—it was 5 am, and she and the people in the church had been waiting half an hour for him to turn up.

I can't think of any woman more likely to put the fear of God into a person at that time of the morning than Cho's redoubtable mother-in-law. He jumped out of bed, dashed to the bathroom for the hastiest of ablutions, grabbed his coat and his Bible and ran to the church. As soon as he rushed on to the platform the whole congregation burst out laughing. He had no time to laugh himself as his mother-in-law advanced rapidly and brusquely pushed him off the platform. He wondered what on earth was the matter; she soon enlightened him.

'Look at you!' He looked down and to his horror found that in his hurry he had put on his coat but was still clad in his pyjama pants! He made another lightning exit, this time in the reverse direction back home to get properly dressed.

It takes a great man to tell such stories against himself. Cho is truly such a man, with a delightful sense of humour; and the Koreans are a fantastic race who enjoy a good laugh. Such a balance is essential when praying is taken so seriously; it is an effective antidote against fanaticism. Happy indeed are the people whose pastor has learned not to take himself too seriously.

5

The Miracle of Triumphant Suffering

The origin of the Korean dawn prayer meetings can be traced back to the great revival of 1907 and to one of the first Korean pastors, Kil Sun-Joo. His is but one of the names of a select band of early Korean Christian leaders, men and women of outstanding valour who laid the foundation of the faith, heroes of the cross, akin to those in Old Testament times who were listed as David's mighty men (2 Sam 23:8–39); names still honoured by Korean Christians of all denominations and who deserve wider recognition.

Kil Sun-Joo was born in a very poor home in Anju on 15th March 1869. As a teenager he became a travelling market trader but without much success, and he took to drinking and gambling. A friend introduced him to Buddhism as the way to succeed in life, and he took it up so earnestly that in 1892 he entered a Buddhist monastery. For three years he concentrated on prayer and meditation, neglecting sleep and keeping himself awake by dousing himself with water. However, all he succeeded in doing was to seriously damage his eyesight; the spiritual power he desired eluded him. He left the monastery and took up the study of Oriental medicine, setting up a shop in Pyongyang. After five years his eyesight deteriorated to the point where he was almost blind, being unable to read even with the strongest lenses. In the meantime, his friend who introduced him to Buddhism had become a Christian and searched him out to tell him the good news. Kil Sun-Joo was in the depths of despair and took some time to be convinced that this 'new faith' could do anything for him; nevertheless, at the insistence of his friend he agreed to go and see the missionary, the Revd Graham Lee. The timing was perfect and Kil Sun-Joo accepted Christ as his Lord and Saviour. Immediately he went back to his little home town of Anju to share his new-found faith with his parents and friends, and his mission was successful. His evangelistic gift was apparent from the beginning and in due time, though his shop was prospering, he left it to become an evangelist, travelling round the Pyongyang and Whanghai provinces.

An eye operation by a missionary doctor helped somewhat, but Kil Sun-Joo's sight remained very poor. In 1903 he was one of the first students to enter the newly established Presbyterian Theological Seminary in Pyongyang. The course lasted for five years, but the successful system adopted was three months of study and nine months out in the field as lay pastors in churches, with self-study work assigned for them to pursue and on which they were examined. He was one of the first seven graduates to complete and be ordained in 1907. Within a month he was installed as the pastor of the Pyongyang Central Presbyterian Church, where he remained for twenty years. His outstanding ministry was largely responsible for it becoming one of the most famous churches in the nation and known as Changdae Hyon Church. This was the church in which the 1907 revival started.

Kil Sun-Joo made it his practice to rise early for prayer. His friend Pak Chi-Rok began joining him for this early morning time of waiting on God. They were so blessed that they brought the matter before the whole church and it was agreed to open it to all who wished to join them for a few days at 4.30 am. The church bell was rung at dawn, but long before then people started to assemble, some as early as 1 am, others at 2 am, and by 4.30 am more than 400 had assembled. It continued not just for a few days and not only in this one church but was taken up by other churches everywhere, and eighty years later, especially in the rural areas, it remains a feature of Korean Christianity.

In the revival, even in the depths of winter which can be very cold in the northern parts, it was a common occurrence for scores and scores of Korean Christians to go out after the evening meeting, kneel on the frozen ground and cry to God for the outpouring of his Holy Spirit and for the salvation of the lost. It is small wonder that with such praying the whole nation was affected.

However, even at the height of the revival there were plenty of problems for the young Korean church. The Japanese, having made Korea a protectorate in 1905, increasingly made their presence felt. There was a long-standing hatred of many centuries between the Koreans and the Japanese, and the missionaries found themselves in a particularly difficult situation. The revival was undoubtedly God's answer, and enabled many Koreans to repent of their bitterness and pray for their enemies. But it was not easy, especially when Japanese soldiers burned down church buildings and added to their outrages by seizing believers, tying them to stakes and shooting them in cold blood. Sometimes God intervened in miraculous ways. Christians escaped what seemed certain death, and faith was strengthened.

The abdication of the Korean emperor in 1907, however, really brought things to a head in the nation, and many Koreans openly revolted and resorted to guer-rilla warfare against the Japanese. A movement called the Righteous Army began in the Wipeng region and it spread like wildfire. In spite of great pressures for Christians to join such freedom fighters, they refused, believing that the church as a spiritual movement must keep aloof from politics. The pressure was particularly strong around

Pyongyang, which was noted for its famous fighters. Pastor Kil Sun-Joo with great courage and wisdom, and by impressing on the Christians that the word of God teaches that 'the powers that be are ordained of God', managed to dissuade them from joining in an insurrection, so avoiding what would have been a useless bloodbath with no hope of success.

As a direct consequence of this policy, the four momentous years which followed the revival saw the great traditions established which became the special feature of Korean Christianity and gave it the needed inspiration to endure the long years of suffering which lay ahead. On 22nd August 1910 Japan formally annexed Korea, and this signalled a further intensification of humiliation and suffering for the nation in general and for the church in particular.

During the forty years of Japanese occupation between 1905 and 1945, some five million Koreans were driven abroad by the oppression, most of them escaping to the north into the vast expanses of Manchuria in north-east China. A further two million were taken to various parts of Japan to be exploited in the mines and mills. As the total population of Korea was then only about twenty million, it meant that over one-third of the population was out of the country. However, in this as in everything else the sovereign overruling hand of God was at work, because these scattered Koreans gained a wider view of the world. Not only that, but Korean churches sprang up in Manchuria, Siberia and even in Japan. These churches were completely independent of any Western missionaries.

The years between 1910 and 1919 were increasingly difficult for the Korean church and for the missionaries. Japan was determined fully to control Korea, not only militarily but socially, educationally and religiously as well. The first target was the church, and they tried to 'Japanize' it and bring it under the control of the Japanese church. They were suspicious of the missionaries (of whom most were Americans) and regarded them as foreign agents. They opened many schools and by various means made it difficult for the mission schools to continue or to compete. Christians were falsely accused, arrested and tortured.

In spite of everything, faithful pastors like Kil Sun-Joo continued to preach, pray and shepherd their people. In 1919 the Korean Declaration of Independence was drawn up and Pastor Kil was one of the thirty-three signatories. With the ending of the First World War, Korean hopes were raised of gaining their independence, and they sought by peaceful means to bring their cause before the nations of the world. The Declaration and the demonstration in Korea on 1st March 1919 were planned secretly by the Koreans and took not only the Japanese by surprise but the missionaries as well. At 2 pm on the appointed day the Declaration was read in public to crowds of many thousands who had gathered. As if by magic, long-banned Korean flags appeared everywhere. The Japanese reacted savagely. Soon the prisons were crowded with those arrested, a disproportionate number of whom were Christians, and some deaths occurred. Kil Sun-Joo was one of the leaders arrested and thrown into prison for three years. For the first year he was kept in solitary confinement but he spent the time in prayer, and in spite of his near blindness read his Bible and memorised the whole Book of Revelation. In the years afterwards he taught this book at Bible conferences without any notes, wholly from memory and with great power. When his period of solitary confinement ended, along with other Christians he turned his imprisonment into an opportunity for evangelism, and many fellow prisoners were won to Christ.

Because fifteen of the thirty-three signatories were Christians, the Japanese were convinced that the church was politically involved and they took swift and terrible vengeance. Christian villages were raided and churches burned. In Suwon the church was set on fire while the people were still in it, and when they tried to escape they were mown down by the Japanese soldiers. Those who remained sang 'Nearer my God to Thee' as the flames enveloped them, and to this day that hymn is sung with great feeling in all Korean churches; it has become something of a Christian national anthem.

Politically the Independence Movement did not bring freedom to Korea, but it did serve to identify the church with the rest of the Korean people in a new and closer way. When Kil Sun-Joo was released he returned to his pastorate and remained there until 1927, when he resigned to become an itinerant preacher. His preaching was always biblical and Christ-exalting. Fittingly, his last service was preaching at a dawn gathering in 1935; he suffered a stroke and died the following day. Thousands attended his funeral. He was typical of hundreds of Korean pastors of that period: a real man of God.

In the 1930s the Japanese did their utmost to undermine the Korean church by imposing Shinto shrine worship upon the nation. All the Korean churches suffered and it was a severe trial. Shinto is the doctrine that the Japanese people, particularly the emperors, are directly descended from the sun-goddess, whom the Japanese call 'Ama-terasu'. This had the effect of making the Japanese feel they were a superior, even a divine, race. The emperor was supposed to be a god and the spirits of the departed emperors of their sun-goddess ancestress were worshipped in the great national shrines in Tokyo and other places. Prayers of adoration were offered at these shrines, and the Japanese erected them in the towns and villages of Korea as well as in the cities and set out to enforce Shinto worship.

In 1935 the Japanese ordered the Christian students in Pyongyang to regularly worship at the Shinto shrine. In November 1935 Dr G F McCune, Headmaster of the Soongshil Junior College, and Mrs V V Snook, Headmistress of the Soongeui Girls' High School, courageously rejected the Japanese order. The Japanese governor gave them sixty days to reconsider, otherwise they would lose their educational qualifications. Ancestor worship had been a part of Korean life for centuries and the Christians had already faced that issue, declaring that it was incompatible with New Testament Christianity. When the Korean Christian leaders considered the very similar issue of the Shinto shrines with the missionaries, they declared their determination to resist Shinto worship no matter what it cost. Within three months such pressure was put upon Dr McCune that he was virtually forced to leave the country. The Japanese even brought Christian leaders over from Japan to try to persuade the Koreans that it was perfectly in order for Christians to participate in the ceremonies at Shinto shrines.

A few Christians cracked under the pressure and yielded, but the many stood firm. Hundreds of Christians were tortured and imprisoned. With the entry of Japan into the Second World War things deteriorated still further. Over 200 churches were closed, over 2,000 Christians were imprisoned and more than 50 church workers suffered martyrdom. It was costly to be a Christian in Korea in those days.

Life under the Japanese was difficult for all Koreans; and every year the pressure increased. They replaced all Koreans in places of influence with Japanese. The teachers were Japanese, and in 1938 even the Korean language was banned: all the children had to learn Japanese. They even imposed Japanese surnames upon families; it was all very humiliating. A few of the teachers were reasonable but the majority were military personnel and very cruel. The towns and cities were renamed; Korean dress was replaced with Japanese attire; and Korean history was banished from the curriculum. The Japanese confiscated almost everything made of metal for the war effort.

As the war progressed and gradually turned against the Japanese, the Koreans felt the full fury of their cruelties. By 1945 it was clear to the Japanese that defeat was near, but the Koreans for the most part were kept in ignorance of the war news. They were, however, commanded to pray for a Japanese victory 'over the barbaric Americans with long noses'. Photos of the divine Japanese emperor were distributed everywhere, even to Christian churches, and people were ordered to bow to it. Any refusal met with swift vengeance. A church in the Kyng Nam area was set on fire and Japanese soldiers stood round it while inside the brave Christians sang. The doors were locked and guarded, but a woman managed to get to a window on the side of the church and tried to push her baby out to safety. Immediately one of the soldiers saw it he ran forward and prodded it back into the inferno within. The singing lessened and moans increased as death mercifully intervened. The smell of burning flesh hung over the area for days.

Children from the local school, who had been working all day in the fields helping to grow food for the war effort, witnessed this scene of carnage as they passed by on the lorry taking them home. Their hatred and fear of the dreaded Japanese increased. A few days later on their way to school they picked up leaflets in Korean and English which had been dropped by the thousand from one of the allied planes. The message implied that deliverance from Japan was at hand. In school their teachers were more and more cruel and punishment for even the most trivial things was extremely harsh. One of the worst teachers was an army corporal; the little boys and girls of eight and nine years of age were terrified of him. But when another allied plane actually flew over the school in broad daylight and dropped more leaflets, the little children could not contain their wonderment and admiration.

One extremely skinny nine-year-old boy forgot his fear for a moment and dared to express his admiration of this

fine plane, even going so far as to mimic its impressive
movements with his arms in the way typical of boys everywhere. Suddenly a more immediate roar claimed their
attention as the corporal teacher marched out into the
playground and took the scene in at a glance. Livid with
rage, he ordered them back into the classroom. Once
inside he barked at the boy who had imitated the plane,
and told him to come out to the front. All the class cringed
in their seats. The corporal suddenly swiped at the hapless
boy with the back of his hand and sent him sprawling to
the floor, blood streaming from his mouth. As he lay there
the tyrant of a teacher jumped on him, once, twice, three
times. To cap this monstrous treatment he then deliberately braced himself against his desk, positioned his boots
on the boy's stomach and chest, and proceeded to lecture
the remainder of the terrified class while standing on the
boy. His tirade over, the corporal, still not satisfied,
pressed his heel deep into the boy's stomach. The little
boy's eyes bulged, his thin arms thrashed the air as he
fought for the breath that would not come, while the
teacher looked on and laughed, enjoying every moment
of his victim's torture. No sooner had the boy managed a
few gasping, painful breaths than the corporal teacher
spat in his face before marching out of the building.

His classmates gathered around the little boy but it was
something neither he nor they would ever forget. Hatred
of the Japanese burned in their hearts. Physically the boy
was permanently damaged, his heart and lungs affected.
It would take not one miracle but many miracles and
many years for him to physically recover from that horren-
dous experience. It would take an even bigger miracle
and even more years for him to get the hatred of the
Japanese out of his heart. But both happened eventually,
for that bruised and broken little boy was none other than
Yonggi Cho.

Shortly after that terrible happening the Second World
War ended and VJ Day was celebrated with as much joy

in Seoul as in London and Washington. 1945 marked the end of Korea's suffering under her Japanese oppressor, but more dreadful years lay ahead for Korea, and for Yonggi Cho and the Korean church.

6

The Miracle of Martyrs

It was Tertullian of Carthage in the third century who said, 'The blood of the martyr is the seed of the church'. An ample supply of martyr seed has not been lacking in the comparatively short existence of the Korean church. Such seed is costly but amazingly fruitful, and that is another reason behind Korea's spectacular church growth.

There was not a day during the forty years that the Japanese occupied Korea but that some Christians were in prison for their faith, and many were martyred during that time. On the day Korea was liberated in 1945, more than 3,000 Korean Christians were released from prison. The leaders of the Grand Alliance had promised in 1943, at the Cairo Declaration, that when the Second World War was won they would ensure that Korea would become free and independent. Although the allies celebrated victory in Europe on 8th May 1945, the war in the Pacific still ground on, with Japan fighting a grim rearguard action. Even as late as July 1945, the American forces in particular were still very concerned about the problem of invading mainland Japan. In addition, they knew that the Japanese armies in Korea and Manchuria still constituted formidable fighting units, and they were more than happy to leave that area of conflict to the Russian army.

The dropping of the two atomic bombs on Japan on 6th and 9th August 1945 suddenly changed the whole situation and brought Japan to the brink of surrender, which came on 15th August. Up to that time America had not had any real long-term interest in Korea, but almost overnight their thinking changed. They reached a hasty decision that it would be wise for them to share in the occupation of Korea. Looking at a wall map, some of the American staff officers noted that the 38th parallel seemed to divide the country fairly evenly in two, and south of this line there was the Korean capital, plus the best agricultural land and a good proportion of the country's light industry. The Russians readily accepted this proposal, which was fortunate because the Americans were in no position to enforce it. The Russian forces were sweeping through Manchuria and they could easily have occupied the whole of Korea before the arrival of any Americans. As it was they dutifully halted at the 38th parallel and another month passed before the Americans landed.

From the very beginning, and especially since the great 1907 revival, the church had been strongest in North Korea, centring around Pyongyang. With the defeat of the Japanese, the Christians in that area emerged in strength and set about rebuilding their church premises, and at great sacrifice erecting new places of worship. They made maximum use of the short time that elapsed between the withdrawal of the Japanese and the arrival of the Russians.

The Christians had many fears but their hopes were high. The dawn prayer meetings were crowded out, outnumbering even the great days of the 1907 revival. As the crowds could not be contained in the buildings, they prayed outside, and gatherings of over 10,000 were witnessed, with all of them once again demonstrating the Korean phenomenon of vast crowds praying aloud simultaneously. The Christians had particular problems of their own to face. It was decided that those ministers who had compromised their faith under the Japanese by participating in the Shinto shrine worship should not be allowed to preach until they had served a period of discipline. It was painful but necessary; if the church was to be strong it must be clean and free from compromise.

It was not envisaged by the United Nations that the division of Korea at the 38th parallel would be permanent. The thinking was that this would pertain only until arrangements had been worked out for a government to rule the whole country. The Russians had other ideas, and they set about organising the northern part of the country so as to make the arrangement permanent, and with definite thoughts of taking over the southern area as well in due course. As customary with communism, they made glowing promises: true freedom would now come to Korea, the many farming abuses suffered under the Japanese would be righted and everyone would have enough land to support themselves and their families.

For a few short months hopes ran high. In Pyongyang the Presbyterians forged ahead with ambitious plans for growth, including the establishing of a seminary to train workers to fill the gaps left by those who had died in prison. As early as September 1945 the Christians had organised the first political party in the country, to stand for democracy and the reformation of society according to Christian ideals. In each district a branch was formed with the church as a centre, and it soon became so strong as to worry the Soviets. They set about organising their own opposition, and soon there was open conflict. After one meeting at a factory an elder was beaten to death, others were injured and the church building damaged. The students (the majority of whom were Christians) began to demonstrate against these outrages but the Soviet authorities reacted savagely, and many students were shot. Before the end of November 1945, the communists were putting pressure on the church. Spies infiltrated the services, arrests became frequent and many either died in prison or disappeared without trace. The communists arranged elections and important meetings, at which attendance was compulsory, on Sundays, to clash with church services.

An extreme communist puppet government was eventually installed under the fanatical and dictatorial Kim Il-Sung who, once he gained power, wielded it ruthlessly and selfishly for himself and his family. Most of the Christians boycotted the election. In 1948 the communists nationalised all property and confiscated all church buildings and religious temples, turning them into warehouses, day-care and retreat centres. Those who were able fled to South Korea, but escape was not easy with Russian and North Korean troops patrolling the new border separating North from South. Every passing year the communists increased their persecution of the Christians. They formed a so-called Christian League and any church workers who would not join were put in prison. By 1950 the communists had achieved their objective and to all intents and purposes had taken over the churches and imprisoned those who would not submit. Those who could not flee went underground. It was surely no coincidence that Pyongyang, which had been at the very heart of the great Korean revival, should be the place to bear the brunt of the attack of godless communism (backed by both Russia and Red China). One of the main objectives seemed to be to destroy every vestige of the Christian faith.

One day the full story of Christian heroism in North Korea during the period from 1945 to 1950 will be told, and it will be one to match the sufferings of the early church under the terrible Roman persecution. Some Christian leaders were crucified and hung on their crosses for days until they died in torment. Christians who persisted in witnessing had their tongues cut out. Even the children were not spared; some who were caught at a secret Sunday School were deliberately deafened by having chopsticks pushed into their eardrums.

Meanwhile, even in South Korea the period 1945–50 was not without its traumas. The Americans had not really 'done their homework' beforehand and consequently they made many blunders. The first Americans landed at Inchon, the major port to Seoul, on 8th September, 1945. After an understandable hesitancy through being subjected to years of anti-American propaganda by the Japanese, the South Koreans gave them a warm welcome. By the time the American vanguard arrived in Seoul they were overwhelmed by the reception they received: cheering Koreans lined the streets, while others hung from every vantage point on buildings. It took longer than it should have done for the Americans to fully appreciate how much the Koreans had suffered at the hands of the Japanese and just what their liberation meant to them.

One of the initial problems was the language: very few Koreans spoke any English, and even fewer of the Americans spoke any Korean, and so the Americans fell into the trap of using Japanese officials who could speak English. These Japanese civil administrators were only too glad to ingratiate themselves with the Americans in any way possible, to avoid punishment for their many misdeeds. The Americans also found the Japanese easier to deal with than the Koreans who, being headstrong and fiercely independent, proved difficult to get along with as well as hard to understand linguistically. This was unfortunate, because the hard facts were that in the three weeks between the Japanese surrender on 15th August and the arrival of the American troops, the Japanese had looted, and deliberately done their utmost to undermine the Korean economy by printing debased currency and other such actions.

It took the Americans many months before they even began to understand the Korean people. Small wonder they were bemused: the capital of the country was still in the horse and cart era, and the few motor vehicles to be found were charcoal-powered. It was like turning the clock back fifty years. On top of all this, many Korean leaders suddenly appeared, all claiming to be the legitimate government of the country. It was all very confusing.

However, even amidst this chaos the Christians gave priority to restoring their churches and reorganising the work in the light of their new-found freedom. It was becoming more and more apparent every passing month that the communists were setting up a repressive regime in the North, and given half a chance they would also take over the South. The only hope of freedom seemed to be for South Korea to become an independent republic, and the church had a vital role to play in this. The Christians were the only ones who, because of their church life, had any experience of democracy, and they were quickly at the forefront of many positive efforts to build a new nation in South Korea.

In the first few years after the Second World War, it was much the same in Korea as in Europe—food and materials were in short supply and life was hard. Nevertheless, with faith and love Christians achieved the seemingly impossible. Especially active were the many Christians who had fled from the North at the first opportunity. The Revd Han Kyung-Chik, with twenty-seven Christian refugees from the North, founded the now world-famous Young Nak Presbyterian Church in 1945. He secured land in the centre of Seoul and began to build. The dawn prayer meeting was started, and it is said that for twenty-five years Dr Han never missed the 5 am prayer time. The increasing influx of deeply committed, praying, refugee believers from the North greatly strengthened the church in South Korea during this crucial period.

In 1948, Syngman Rhee was elected the president of South Korea. His name has become surrounded with

controversy, but compared with the communist tyrant in
the North, Kim Il-Sung, he was a saint. Syngman Rhee
(born 1875) was a zealous patriot, and before he became
a Christian he was a freedom fighter in the early days of
the Japanese occupation at the beginning of the century.
For these activities he was blacklisted by the Japanese
and was constantly having to go into hiding to escape
arrest. When at last the Japanese did catch up with him
he was condemned to death. In a small cell he waited,
expecting every day to be his last. Some years previously
he had raised money by giving language lessons to American missionaries. Hearing of his arrest, the missionaries
prayed very specially for him, and when he sent them,
from his condemned cell, a request for a Bible and a
dictionary, they readily complied. Facing death all alone
in his cramped and airless cell, the message of the Bible
went straight to his heart. For the first time in his life he
prayed and called upon God to save his soul and his
country. He had a genuine conversion experience about
which many Korean Christians have no doubt. He
witnessed to the warder and then to the warder's brother,
and won them both for Christ.

The change in him was so real that when he asked for
permission to start a Bible class among the other prisoners, it was granted. The warder's brother eventually
entered the ministry. Instead of being executed, Syngman
Rhee was released and allowed to leave the country. He
went to America where he studied at both Harvard and
Princeton, obtaining his MA and PhD. Apart from a short
visit to his homeland in 1910, he spent the next thirty-
five years in America—but he never forgot his country
and campaigned relentlessly for Korea's independence. It
was undoubtedly to his advantage that he was out of
Korea for so long; his rivals in the election in 1948 were
all at loggerheads with each other, and he at least could
not be accused of collaborating with the Japanese in any
way. Although there were some unanswered questions

about the election, and the weeks in the run-up to it were filled with violence in which 589 people lost their lives, the UN Commissioners were satisfied as to its validity.

Syngman Rhee was inaugurated as president on 24th July 1948. He was a Methodist, and some of the top posts in his government were also filled by committed Christians; many pastors also became district governors. It is easy to criticise Syngman Rhee but he had an extremely difficult task on his hands. Strong government was essential. The communists in the North were doing all they could to foster revolution in the South, in preparation for a complete take-over of the whole country. Political rivals were imprisoned and ruthless measures were taken by Syngman Rhee; undoubtedly he was dictatorial, but no one can question his patriotism—he wanted a free and independent Korea. Yet there were many factions and the Christians were still very much in the minority.

There were many local uprisings, some of which produced Christian martyrs whose stories stirred the country and strengthened the resolve of the government as well as the church. One of the most moving incidents concerned the two young sons of an outstanding Christian minister, the Revd Son Yang-Won, who had taken a very strong stand on the Shinto shrine issue and was imprisoned by the Japanese for this until liberation came in 1945. On his release he returned to his work among the lepers in the extreme south of the country at Yosu. There was a military training camp in the area which was the scene of a cleverly organised communist uprising in the spring of 1948. The communists actually succeeded in taking over the whole of the surrounding area for a short time, in which they created mayhem. They set up their notorious people's courts and hauled landowners and Christians before them for 'instant judgement'.

The Revd Son Yang-Won had two sons at the Yosu High School who were living with a family in the town.

The boys were both committed believers and recognised as such in the town. Friends knew they would be likely targets for the communists and urged them to flee, but they refused although they understood the danger they were in. They did not go to school but chose to remain in their lodgings. In the middle of the morning a crowd of communist students surrounded the house. They then dragged them out and proceeded to beat the older boy, saying that they were going to knock this Christian religion out of him. Next they hauled them off to the communist headquarters, where the boys found themselves confronted with the corpses of many who had already been shot on the orders of the people's court.

The leader of the group, called An Chae-Son, threatened the two boys with a revolver and told them that unless they recanted of their faith they would be shot. The younger boy, Tong-Sin, actually tried to protect his older brother, Tong-In, but Tong-In insisted that the communists only wanted to kill him and urged his younger brother to go home and care for their parents.

His captors then blindfolded Tong-In who testified of his faith in Christ before An Chae-Son shot him. Tong-Sin rushed forward and embraced the body of his martyred brother. He then proceeded to urge them all to repent of what they had done and accept Jesus as their saviour. This only enraged them still more and they killed Tong-Sin also, the bodies of the two brothers lying side by side.

When news of what had happened reached their godly father, he went into the church and prayed, thanking God for the honour of being the father of two such brave young martyrs, and beseeching God for grace to forgive their murderer and for mercy upon him. The funeral was a great witness and the forgiving attitude of the father impressed many.

Very shortly afterwards the mutiny was quelled and the town returned to normal again. When the father sent word by his daughter to the authorities asking for mercy for the murderer of his two sons, the colonel in charge was speechless. He was so baffled by this extraordinary request that he felt he must see the father for himself. With the accused prisoner An Chae-Son securely tied, he drove out to meet the father and asked him, was it really true that he wanted the life of this his sons' murderer to be spared? Face to face for the first time with the accused, without hesitation this godly man replied:

'My sons were ready to die, for they were Christians. This one is not ready because he does not know the Lord Jesus. Please turn him over to me, I want to tell him of the love of the Lord Jesus for him. At least give him a stay of execution. I shall send a request for pardon to President Syngman Rhee, whom I know personally.'

The colonel was impressed and deeply moved, acknowledging that he had never before met such love as this. He agreed to turn the boy over to the father, but he would have to accept full responsibility for him.

The first thing the Revd Son Yang-Won did was to take the young man to his parents to explain why he had pleaded for their son's life to be spared. He told them of what Jesus had done in dying for sinners on the cross at Calvary and of God's amazing grace. Right there in that room he had the joy of leading both the parents and their son to Christ. The newly converted parents wanted to express their gratitude in a tangible way and they offered to take the Revd Son Yang-Won's daughter into their home, with a dual purpose in mind: they wanted to care for her but they also wanted her to instruct them in their new-found faith. An Chae-Son was taken into Son Yang-Won's home, and later enrolled in the seminary in Pusan to train for Christian work.

This story stirred the nation. It was fully told in a book entitled *Love's Atom Bomb*. In addition, some Christian young people formed a drama group and went from town to town presenting the story in dramatised form. Every performance finished with the gospel being explained and an invitation extended to accept Jesus Christ as saviour. Thousands responded as once again the costly but fruitful martyr seed was sown in the land. Little did they dream that two years later the nation was to be plunged into a most bloody war, in which hundreds more would share the fate of these two young martyrs.

7

The Miracle of a Second Visitation

At 4 am on the Sunday morning of 25th June 1950, North Korea launched its invasion of South Korea with a devastating artillery and mortar barrage which took the South completely by surprise. There had been intelligence rumours as far back as 1949, as relations between the two sections of the divided nation deteriorated. Serious incidents along the 38th parallel escalated dangerously, but America and the free world tended to dismiss the idea of invasion by the North as extremely unlikely. They took the view that such a happening may occur in the distant future, but for the present the communists were following their usual tactics of seeking to foster revolution inside the South by widespread underground activity.

By the time the Christians were flocking into their churches for the early services that fateful Sunday, the North Korean soldiers were pouring over the border at an alarming rate. The Russians had withdrawn from North Korea and the Americans had all but completed the evacuation of their forces from South Korea. The main difference was that the Russians had left the ruthless North Korean president Kim Il-Sung with a formidable fighting force of 135,000 men. These comprised seven combat-ready divisions, equipped with Russian T–34 tanks, heavy artillery and backed up with an air force of fighters and ground-attack bombers. The Americans had left Syngman Rhee with an army of 95,000 men, but devoid of tanks, anti-tank weapons and heavy artillery; their only air force was a few T–6 trainers. They also lacked adequate stores of ammunition and vehicle spares. The policy was for a peace-time army rather than one geared for aggression.

It seems certain that Kim Il-Sung had persuaded the Russians that he could attack and take over South Korea before the Americans would be able to intervene. Within four days, on 29th June, the North Korean army was in Seoul and the South Korean army was retreating in total disarray. It seemed very much as though Kim Il-Sung's forecast was going to prove correct. Furthermore, it was soon very clear that the Christians were a principal target for the communists. The invasion had taken place so quickly that many church leaders were caught and killed; others were taken prisoner and carried away. Those who stayed in Seoul hid as best they could. Some survived, but many were discovered and lost their lives. During the next few weeks the whole future of free Korea and the Korean church hung in the balance.

The Americans and South Koreans soon discovered that they were dealing with a cruel and merciless foe to whom life was cheap. Bodies of captured soldiers (American and South Korean) were discovered with their hands tied behind their backs (in some cases fastened with barbed wire) and shot. The normal conventions of war were not observed. Just when everything seemed lost, however, several vital things happened which as surely revealed the overruling providence of Almighty God as Dunkirk did in the dark days of 1940 when Britain's future likewise hung by a thread.

As soon as it was established that North Korea had invaded South Korea, an emergency meeting of the United Nations Security Council was called in New York at Lake Success. Because of the time difference, New York being almost half a day behind Seoul, it was still only the afternoon of Sunday 25th June when the Security Council met. The Russian delegate had walked out of the Council six months previously in protest at the UN's refusal to allow Red China into the United Nations in place of Chiang Kai Shek's Nationalist China. Yakov Malik, the Russian delegate, was still absent on 25th June. At 6 pm the UN Security Council unanimously passed a resolution condemning the North Korean aggression and calling for them to withdraw immediately. The vote was nine for, none against. Because of the Russian absence it was a unique happening. Max Hastings in his brilliant book *The Korean War* says of the vote: 'It was a landmark event, probably never to be repeated in the history of this, or any other world body. The UN intervention was a fluke of history, made possible by the unique accident of the Russian boycott.' Many Christians, especially those in Korea, would see it rather as the overruling, sovereign hand of God.

From the outset, America's President Truman was determined to resist North Korea's aggression. Strengthened by the UN Security Council's resolution, he ordered General MacArthur in Japan to provide the South Korean army with ammunition and equipment, as well as the support of the American navy and air force. Even MacArthur, who was always a law unto himself, was amazed at the way this immense decision was taken by the president without any submission to Congress. The decision came as an equal shock to Moscow and Peking, who had not anticipated such a strong and courageous reaction from the United States. The US then proceeded to rally support from Britain and the other free nations. General MacArthur, the hero of the Pacific War against Japan, although now seventy years of age, was appointed as supreme commander of the UN force. Help began to arrive in Korea almost immediately, but even so things were precarious to say the least. American planes flew supplies to an airstrip on the southern tip of Korea, but even as General MacArthur flew in on 29th June for his first visit to view the situation for himself, a communist fighter plane attacked his plane and had to be driven off by the escorting American Mustang fighter planes.

The American soldiers flown over from the army of occupation in Japan were not really prepared for combat, nor was there time to train them up to combat readiness. After the victorious culmination of the Second World War in 1945, America and her allies had all had more than enough of war, and their main concern was to run down their armed forces and get their wartime conscripts demobilised and back home to 'civvy street'. Now, five years later, they were forced to face up to the growing menace of world domination by communism. The rise of Red China, the world's biggest nation by far, alongside Red Russia, had really set the alarm bells ringing, especially in Washington. President Harry Truman grasped the nettle and committed his great nation to the conflict against communism. He and his advisors suddenly realised the strategic importance of Korea, and once stirred they acted with the usual genius of America for 'getting things organised and getting things done'. Even so, time was against them; the North Korean army was driving south and brushing aside all opposition with embarrassing ease.

The desperate need was to delay the advance of the enemy long enough for reinforcements to be brought in. The American air force poured thousands of tons of bombs on the areas occupied by the enemy, but with little effect. In the first few weeks of the war such chaos and confusion reigned that, because there were no means of effective communication between the South Korean ground forces and the American air force, many bombs fell into empty rice paddy fields. Worse still, not a few bombs were inadvertently dropped on positions still held by the South Koreans, with resultant casualties and a further drop in morale. The first few American units to be thrown into the battle had no time to accustom themselves to either the unique terrain of the country or the terrifyingly effective tactics of the enemy before they too were flung back and forced to join the endless flood of refugees filling all roads south. More than once, Americans holding a vital position beside a road would see a group of weary refugees shuffling towards them, then suddenly at the last minute these would be swept aside to reveal North Korean soldiers using them as cover. It was frightening and brutalising to be thrown in unprepared to face a ruthless enemy brainwashed into suicidal assaults with complete disregard for their own lives.

By the beginning of August the Americans were reduced to grimly endeavouring to keep a toe-hold in Korea, as for six weeks they waged the famous 'battle of the Pusan perimeter', the area right at the south-east tip of the Korean peninsular. They all knew that if the North Koreans succeeded in driving them completely out of Korea, it would be a long and dangerous task to ever get back in again. The first British brigade had arrived, but they also were so poorly equipped that they were soon being called 'the Woolworth Brigade'. In many ways it was a crisis comparable to Dunkirk. The difference was that on this occasion the troops under General Walker's command somehow withstood the fanatical and suicidal onslaughts of Kim Il-Sung's army just long enough for another near-miracle to happen.

The man responsible for making the near-miracle possible was General Douglas MacArthur. The legendary hero showed once again his unique charisma and daring by attempting what everyone else on his general staff said was impossible. He alone believed that he could take the enemy by surprise by landing a force at the great port of Inchon on the west coast, just a few miles from Seoul and behind the North Koreans' present lines. Never a man to be indecisive, once he had secured the reluctant backing of his chiefs of staff he set about implementing the bold, imaginative and dangerous plan. Because Inchon's tidal range was the highest in the world, there were only three dates when the tide would be high enough for a landing: 15th and 27th September, and 11th October. There were other major difficulties also, including the fact that the typhoon season was upon them.

Nevertheless the plan went ahead, and a hurriedly assembled force of 260 ships succeeded in safely carrying 70,000 American soldiers through a 125 mph typhoon in readiness for the landing on 15th September. Although tens of thousands were in on the plan, somehow the North Koreans were kept in total ignorance of the venture. Everything went through as planned and a beachhead was established with the amazingly small loss of only twenty lives. On 16th September the drive to Seoul to retake the capital was under way.

The same day, in the south of the country, the beleaguered forces of General Walker were enabled by the diversion created by the Inchon landing to break out of the Pusan perimeter. Now it was the turn of the North Koreans to find themselves in danger of being encircled and cut off. The American forces from Inchon and Pusan linked up on 26th September, but desperate street fighting was witnessed in the devastated capital as 20,000 North Koreans defended stubbornly. Finally they were bombed and shelled out of existence, along with a good deal of those parts of the city which had survived up to that point.

On 29th September General MacArthur presided over the ceremony marking the liberation of Seoul, and handed it over once again to Syngman Rhee and his government. The general was quite sure that the war was as good as won, and all over 'bar the shouting'—and so it seemed for a short time.

The liberators of Seoul were horrified when they discovered the terrible atrocities which the communists had committed during the brief three months of occupation.

They found trenches filled with the bodies of hundreds of men, women and children. The few months in which they were occupied by the North Koreans were more than enough to convince otherwise those South Koreans with communist sympathies. The UN estimated that around 26,000 South Korean civilians were slaughtered in cold blood by the North Koreans between 25th June and 27th September.

The UN forces continued to push the retreating North Koreans back across the 38th parallel, and by 19th October they captured the North Korean capital of Pyongyang. However, before they evacuated Seoul the communists carried out mass executions of Christians and burned many churches. Nevertheless, within a week after the UN troops had freed the city, on the Sunday, some 3,000 Christians gathered for a service in West Gate Church. It was rumoured that Kim Il-Sung had fled to Manchuria and everyone thought that the war was in effect over.

General MacArthur was intent on pushing the battle to the borders of China in the north, and he refused to give any assurances to the Chinese, who after all were not considered a formidable military foe. In the euphoria following the near-miraculous change in the war, after the brilliant landing at Inchon turned the brink of defeat into near rout, rumblings about Chinese intervention were ignored. The UN forces continued their push north, with General MacArthur intent on destroying Kim Il-Sung's army and occupying the whole of North Korea. They were especially anxious to get to the Chosin reservoir and prevent the communists from destroying the vast dams, which were important sources of power. The Christians, however, decided that the wisest direction for them to follow was south, while they had the opportunity. Up to 1945, 75 per cent of Korean Presbyterians lived in the north. About 100,000 Christians, including many pastors who had somehow survived the communist reign of terror, fled South at the end of October 1950. It was as well they did, because a week after the UN forces had taken Pyongyang the Chinese entered the war; far from being over, the war had entered a new and terrible phase.

Quietly, with astonishing secrecy, Mao Tse Tung had ordered his armies to resist 'the US Imperialist aggression' and, as if from nowhere, the UN forces suddenly found themselves overwhelmed by an army of 100,000 fiercely committed Chinese soldiers. As the Korean winter and this new foe both descended on the endless mountains of North Korea, the UN forces were soon in desperate straits. They suffered untold miseries from the savage cold, with night temperatures dropping to twenty below freezing, and they dared not relax because night was the time when the Chinese were especially active. The Chinese seemed not to feel the cold as much or to find the darkness a hindrance to their movements. By 5th December the Chinese had retaken Pyongyang; by Christmas Day they had crossed the 38th parallel and were heading south. New Year's Day 1951 was the signal for a new offensive by the communists, and on 4th January the UN forces had to evacuate Seoul. Once more Christians found themselves trapped, and it was estimated that 500 Christian leaders in Seoul alone were either killed or kidnapped by the communists. Thirty-nine prominent Christian pastors were martyred in Seoul.

The war was now at a terrible stage. The Chinese did not seem to mind suffering heavy casualties, and the UN forces found themselves killing hordes of them only to discover more simply taking their place. The fighting was fierce and bitter with heavy losses on both sides and among the civilians. Such was the scale of the fighting (in what was after all a comparatively small country) that scarcely a Korean family escaped the dreadful privation and suffering which became their common lot during the three long years of the war from 1950 to 1953. Through the long weary months the conflict dragged on, first one side advancing, then the other side pushing them back as further reinforcements were thrown in. The more troops the Chinese threw in, the more the Americans increased their firepower, with bombs and artillery threatening to flatten the very mountains in which the Reds were entrenched.

Literally millions of South Koreans had to flee their homes and live as best they could; scratching an existence, living almost like animals in an endeavour to survive the holocaust. As the war correspondent and author Max Hastings states in *The Korean War:* 'The television comedy show *MASH* (which is the popular awareness) projects an image of the Korean War infinitely less savage' than the real one. 'The UN (mainly Americans but sixteen nations in all including Britain) suffered 142,000 casualties, and the Koreans themselves lost at least a million people. Chinese casualties remain uncertain but they run into many hundreds of thousands.'

After weeks of very heavy fighting the UN forces retook Seoul on 14th March 1951, but they entered a devastated city in which 80 per cent of the buildings were destroyed—the only principal buildings still standing were the Capitol and the railway station. In April the UN forces once more succeeded in pushing the enemy back North over the 38th parallel, only to be flung back themselves as the Chinese launched another offensive which was finally halted just north of Seoul.

After many abortive peace talks and two more years of fighting, the armistice was at last signed at Panmunjom on 27th July 1953. It was estimated that 300,000 Christians had lost their lives in the war, and more than 2,000 church buildings were destroyed. About 1,000 pastors, evangelists and church leaders were lost during the war. There were stories of heroism and courage both in the UN forces (such as the epic stand of the British 29th Brigade at the Imjin River in April 1951) and among the Christians.

The amazing thing was that after the terrible sufferings the Korean Christians who survived were granted a second visitation of the Holy Spirit. This is the only way to account for the growth and strength of the Korean church, which virtually 'came back from the dead' in 1953. Thousands of young Christians enrolled in the seminaries to train for the ministry. Out of 150,000 North Korean prisoners of war, 20,000 were converted. This was a unique happening. Needless to say, these converts did not want to return to North Korea and this became a point of controversy in the peace talks, but on 17th June President Syngman Rhee ordered the South Korean guards to release North Korean prisoners who did not wish to be repatriated.

The further influx of tens of thousands of deeply committed Christians from North Korea during the Korean War greatly strengthened the church in South Korea, and was undoubtedly a factor in the revival. Another factor was the quality of Korean leadership which emerged from the furnace of suffering, men such as Dr Kim Joon-Gon, a Presbyterian minister and currently the national director of Korea Campus Crusade. During the Korean War he was in Chido, which for three months was under the domination of the communists. One night the communists came and murdered his wife and his father before his very eyes; they then proceeded to beat him into unconsciousness with a club. They left him for dead, but somehow he regained his senses and set out to search for his small daughter. During the next few weeks he narrowly escaped death many times. Out of a population of 20,000 the communists killed 2,000 in cold blood. When he found his little girl he could do nothing to help her, because they were both dying with hunger and she was pining for her dead mother.

He confessed that though he was a committed Christian, he was so shattered by what had happened that he stopped praying and soon lapsed into a numbed state of spiritual darkness and despair. Then one day he suddenly found that his lips were moving in prayer; he felt that it was the Holy Spirit beginning the prayer for him. In a matter of moments as he prayed from his heart he was renewed and his soul restored. Christ once again filled his heart with joy and peace. As he emerged from this dark valley experience he felt the Lord calling him to witness to the very communist who had killed his loved ones. He began to pray for this man and God removed the hatred from his heart until he felt courage and boldness to go and tell this man about the love of God in Christ. The communist leader was staggered to find that Kim Joon-Gon was still alive, and when he was told that he had come to him in love and with forgiveness, the communist broke down and wept his way to salvation. Today that man is an elder in a Korean church.

Dr Kim Joon-Gon is just one of the many chosen vessels who, having suffered great things for the cause of Christ, emerged in the post-Korean War era to give vital leadership to the Church. Sons and daughters whose parents had been martyred in North Korea, who made it to the freedom of South Korea, then travelled throughout the nation proclaiming the Jesus for whom their parents had so willingly shed their blood. Life and death, heaven and hell, time and eternity, were very real to these people, as was the Second Coming of Christ. All these things gave an urgency to the gospel which generated the right kind of atmosphere for revival.

Before 1950 not many people had even heard of Korea; the Korean War catapulted this little nation to the centre of the world's stage, and it has never been out of the limelight for very long ever since. Dr Billy Graham visited Korea during the war in December 1952 and preached to the soldiers as well as to the Koreans. He went again in February 1956, and has visited on several other important occasions.

Dr Bob Pierce was another outstanding American preacher who visited Korea before and after the war, and whose films of Korea and his pleas for help on behalf of the tens of thousands of war orphans stirred Christians around the world. His World Vision organisation did marvellous work among the orphans. The Revd Dr Marlin L Nelson came to Korea in 1956 as director of World Vision in Korea and he has been there ever since. A self-effacing and godly man he has given the best years of his life to this nation, and is typical of the new generation of missionaries who have blessed and helped rebuild Korea in the vital period after the war. There was a flood of missionary help as many societies moved into Korea for the first time, such as the American Southern Baptists and the American Assemblies of God.

It would be wonderful to record that everything was perfect in the Korean church at this period, but it would be a false picture. Sadly, as relief money poured in for orphanages, widows' homes and babies' care centres, the temptation proved too much for a small minority of pastors and deacons in trusted positions, and they embezzled support money and used it for their own benefit. Some even used the money for election campaigns to secure seats in the National Assembly. Such happenings caused a public scandal and greatly harmed the cause of Christ in the nation. Nevertheless, the majority of Christian leaders were above reproach. The standard of ministry and training provided was remarkable in the circumstances prevailing at the time, and was indubitably another vital factor in the growth of the church in the immediate post-Korean War period.

In 1941 there was a total of forty churches in Seoul; by 1958 there were 400. It was the same in other cities such as Taegu, where in 1941 there were seven churches and in 1958 there were 170. In the first two years after the end of the Korean War there were 2,000 new church buildings erected. The awakening of 1953, though different in many ways from that of 1907, was just as outstanding, and in the light of all that has happened since it was probably even more remarkable.

8

The Miracle of Signs and Wonders

Concerned Christians everywhere are interested in church growth. It is natural, therefore, that Paul Yonggi Cho as the pastor of the world's largest church is inundated with requests to lecture on this subject. Churches of many denominations write to him from all over the world. He is sad, however, that many of them state that while they want him to lecture on church growth they do not wish him to touch on the supernatural. But he is adamant.

'Signs and wonders are the great secret of church growth in this day and age.'

Sitting with him in his beautiful office on the twelfth floor of the World Mission Centre building, he told me:

'I pray for the sick in every service and always we see God working and confirming his word with signs following.' Healing is an inseparable part of his ministry and something that he does with great faith and compassion, yet without ostentation or showmanship. His preaching is always very positive, faith-building and inspiring, and salvation takes precedence over healing.

In every service we attended when he was preaching, it was deeply moving to see the readiness with which people responded to his appeal for them to accept Jesus Christ as their lord and saviour. His appeals were clear and forthright but devoid of undue pressure, yet all over the great congregation hands were raised, and when he asked them to stand they did so by the score. They were all quickly supplied by the small army of stewards on duty with a decision form to complete. Then and only then did he pray for the sick, so that there was little chance of the issue of salvation being confused with that of healing as can so easily happen in large evangelistic healing crusades.

When he prays for the sick he does so from the platform; the numbers anyway are too great for him to pray and lay hands on each individual. Furthermore, the time schedule in the services is always tight; when you have another 25,000 outside beginning to queue up to make sure that they get into the main sanctuary for the next service, it helps the preacher's 'and finally' to be just that! However, there is never a sense of rush or hurry in any part of the service. Having prayed a general prayer of healing Yonggi Cho frequently manifests a spiritual gift as the Holy Spirit gives to him a word of knowledge about someone being healed of a specific illness at that very moment. Always when such words of knowledge are given the congregation responds positively and vociferously, showing just how much they are all involved in this prayer for the sick.

The apparent ease with which all this is accomplished leaves one questioning whether the results are real. Are folk truly getting saved? Are many, or even any, of these people really being healed? I had gained the impression before I came to Korea that most of the people responding to salvation in the services were in fact only publicly confirming a decision already made in a cell group. Inquiries revealed otherwise. Nearly all of the hundreds responding in the main services are first-time decisions. It is true that a large percentage of them are brought in by the ever-zealous cell leaders, but I discovered the secret behind it. The cell leaders bring them in with confidence because it has been proved by experience that Yonggi

Cho's ministry reaches people at the point of their need. They tell him:

'Pastor, we are thrilled because the sinners we bring to church, you always catch them. This is the reason we are excited. If you were unable to catch them, then we would be discouraged in bringing sinners to church. At least we can help you in this way, in bringing the sinners to church so that you can catch them.' It is a wonderful combined effort. The numbers of those responding who become linked to a cell group and members of the church is proof of a real work of grace in their hearts.

The same applies to the healings. From time to time spectacular miracles occur, but most of the healings happen quietly and without any undue fuss. Although God uses Yonggi Cho so marvellously, he does not claim to have the gift of healing. Faced with very many sick and needy people, especially in the early days of his ministry in the aftermath of the Korean War, he prayed fervently for the gift of healing but did not receive it. His early ambition was to be an evangelist rather than a pastor. Indeed he acknowledges that at first he neglected his church ministry in his consuming desire to become the Billy Graham of Korea. He pursued this desire so relentlessly that he neglected his church, his family and his health, and suffered a major breakdown as a consequence. Laid aside with sickness he sought the face of God, and it was made clear to him that his calling was to be a pastor: that was his gift and he was to settle down and feed the flock of God. Nevertheless, as a pastor he does the work of an evangelist (2 Timothy 4:5), and wins so many souls that he must rank with the greatest evangelists of our day. Obedience is always the key to success in God's work. One of his sayings is: 'God's guidance is never meant to be modified.'

Because Yonggi Cho has suffered so much sickness himself he is extremely sensitive to the needs of others, and this is apparent when he is ministering to the sick. I found his approach to the subject of divine healing to be balanced and free from wild extravagences. He knows only too well that healings are not always immediate, and even when God touches a person they still need wisdom as well as faith if they are to keep their healing.

From childhood Yonggi Cho was always weak and sickly. About a year after the terrible incident in school when the Japanese teacher stood on his chest and stomach, inflicting internal injury, he went down with a severe case of measles. In those days in Korea it was often fatal because of the lack of modern drugs. For weeks the delicate little boy hovered on the brink of death. Day and night his mother and family watched over their precious eldest son, bathing his fever-wracked body and doing their utmost to nurse him back to health. At long last their efforts were rewarded; he turned the corner and slowly recovered, though he remained weak. The next four years were a constant struggle for survival and then, when he was fourteen years of age and in high school, the Korean War broke out.

Food was scarce and malnutrition something all were suffering from, but Yonggi Cho was less able to cope with it than most, and at the time he was finishing his first year in the Technical High School in Busan, illness struck again: one cold winter day he started coughing up blood. By then he was eighteen years old and to help his finances he was doing extra work as a tutor in English (which he was learning as he went along). His parents took him to hospital. The doctors examined him and took X-rays which revealed that both his lungs were severely affected with tuberculosis. It was found that he was also suffering from pleurisy. His family were too poor to pay for treatment, not that the doctors thought it would do him any good as he was really past help and had at most just three months to live. There was no room for him in the overcrowded hospital and no point in admitting someone who was going to die anyway. His family resigned themselves to the situation and he left home to face death alone.

He and his family were still Buddhists—not that Buddha ever seemed to answer any of their many prayers—but one of his four sisters had a friend who was a keen Christian. Hearing about his sad plight this young girl took it upon herself to visit him, although in Korean culture it was an almost unthinkable thing to do: women had no status and he was the eldest son and therefore greatly superior. How dare this eighteen-year-old girl come knocking at his door and presume to speak to a man? To add insult to injury she had a Bible in her hand and was starting to preach to him, a Buddhist, about Jesus. Weak as he was he ordered her out.

When his family learned of her visit they also forbade her to return, but this girl was not repulsed so easily and she returned several times, always pressing the claims of Christ upon him until forced to leave. At last she persuaded him to receive her Bible as a gift and he started to read it. Eventually, through reading the Gospel of Matthew he discovered Christ as his saviour, and as he read on he found him to be the great healer also. He prayed to Jesus and in six months' time he was able to leave his sick-bed and walk quite freely. Then he met with a set-back: he started spitting up blood again. He felt sure that it must be because he had grieved the Lord in some way and he started praying and fasting, which in his still weak condition caused him to feel faint. On the third day of this fast as he was praying in the early hours of the morning it suddenly seemed to him that the whole room was on fire. It was a burning bush experience in which the Lord Jesus appeared to him and solemnly charged him to preach the gospel. He fell asleep and in the morning when he awoke he felt rested. When he opened his mouth to thank the Lord he found himself speaking in a language he did not understand. After this moving experience he prayed with renewed earnestness, and he knew within himself that he was being healed of his tuberculosis.

About a year later, with not even enough possessions to fill a haversack, Yonggi Cho entered the unpretentious Assemblies of God Bible College in Seoul. This was under the auspices of the American Assemblies of God who had moved into Korea after the war. He was so full of zeal for his new-found faith that he overdid things and collapsed. One of his classmates, a mature student, was a registered nurse and she took it upon herself to treat him medically, but more importantly she set herself to pray for him. A married woman with a family and one who knew the secrets of intercessory prayer, she set herself to pray for this young man because she sensed that God's hand was upon him. She prayed for several days until he recovered. Her name was Jashil Choi and she was destined to play an important role in his life.

She began to teach him about prayer, and soon there were five of them in the college rising daily at 4.30 am to wait on God. They made so much noise that the other students in the dormitory objected and tried to stop them as it was interfering with sleep. Yonggi Cho says those five are the only ones out of the fifty students who graduated with him who are still in the ministry today. It was then that he learned how to pray for hours at a time, something which has been the hallmark of God's specially anointed ones through the centuries, such as Luther, Wesley, Whitefield, Finney, Hudson Taylor and the like.

He left Bible College on 18th May 1958, and in conjunction with Dr Jashil Choi he pioneered his first church in an old ex-American army tent at Bulkwang-dong in Seoul. Even though God had healed him of his tuberculosis his heart was very weak and he experienced constant palpitations. At times he was forced to lie down where he was until he recovered sufficiently to carry on. Every day he was compelled to look to the Lord Jesus for strength and help. Nevertheless, even that weak physical state was not allowed to become an excuse for not praying.

I asked Dr Yonggi Cho if he would tell me about the present revival in Korea, and especially about some of the things he would never forget as being times when the Holy Spirit had moved in power. He took me back to his pioneer days in the tent. At the time he and the people in his church virtually lived in the tent, and then in the first building they erected. For three years he stayed there almost night and day, and the people and their families brought their blankets and joined him. Those who had to go to work would leave in the morning and return in the evening to spend most of the night praying together. In those days they had very little sleep, but the presence of God became so real that they were afraid to leave lest they should miss some wonderful happening.

Large areas of the city of Seoul were still devastated after the Korean War and consequently the times were abnormal in very many ways. Because of the shortages endured in the latter part of the Japanese occupation, and the Korean War which followed shortly after, a large percentage of the population suffered with tuberculosis. As Yonggi Cho and his church waited on God in this extended way, the Divine Presence filled the place and they experienced the most wonderful revival, with people being healed from many diseases including tuberculosis and many finding Christ as saviour. He said that obviously such a state of affairs with Christians living in the church twenty-four hours a day could not go on forever, but that was the time when God met them in special power and it is something he will never forget. In just over three years the work grew from 5 to 400 members.

Around this time, in 1961, he was called up to do the two years' military service which was compulsory for all young men. He was drafted into the Intelligence Corps. After a few months he was taken seriously ill and rushed to a military hospital for an emergency operation which lasted eight hours. During the post-operative time in hospital he developed pneumonia and his life was in danger. No penicillin was available and his physical strength was insufficient to pull him through. Once again his friend and colleague Dr Jashil Choi came to his aid. Night and day she stayed by his bedside and prayed. Yonggi Cho firmly believes that her prayers, along with those of his praying people in the church, pulled him through. He was given a medical discharge from the army and returned to his pastorate.

Just before Yonggi Cho was drafted into the army an American missionary, Dr John Hurston, returned to Korea. He had visited in 1958 for evangelistic meetings after a period of missionary service in Africa; Yonggi Cho had acted as his interpreter, and had impressed him very favourably. I was privileged to meet Dr Hurston at the 1981 Assemblies of God General Conference in England when he was a guest speaker along with Dr Yonggi Cho, and I found him to be a true servant of Christ and a man of prayer with a beautiful touch of God on his life.

He befriended Yonggi Cho at a critical period. During the time that Cho was away in the army Dr Hurston came to help Jashil Choi with the tent church, and God blessed his ministry. In one meeting in particular God poured out his Spirit upon them and two hundred new members were added to the church. Even so, they were missing Yonggi Cho. As they prayed for his release from the army, Hurston felt that God gave him a clear revelation that Cho would only be away for seven months. Due to his operation he was given his discharge and returned to Seoul seven months after his call-up. He found that in his absence the church had moved to Sodaemoon, in the West Gate area of the city. Starting with a tent, they soon graduated to a prefabricated structure. This new building was dedicated on 18th February 1962 and some outstanding healings occurred, including that of a cripple who had crawled in and left walking, and a totally deaf man of over sixty years of age who had his hearing restored. Hurston graciously stepped down upon Cho's return, but he stayed on to work with Cho until the 1980s. John Hurston is typical of the fine body of self-effacing missionaries who have worked in the background and allowed the Korean church to develop and mature unhindered.

9

The Miracle of More Miracles

With all ministry the great test is not just starting something but sustaining it. Yonggi Cho's ministry of the miraculous developed rapidly during those pioneer days. Even so, many more trials awaited him, all of which served to widen his understanding of the many mysteries which confront all who enter into this ministry. He was to be criticised as well as praised; opposed as well as supported.

The ministry of healing has always aroused controversy. Healings occurred during the pre-Korean War revival years, but were never really accepted by the main body of believers in Korea, especially the Presbyterians who were (and still are) the largest denomination.

Even Kim Ik-Du, who was the most outstanding revival leader of that pre-war era, eventually dropped healing from his ministry because of the opposition it aroused. This mighty man of God (who lived from 1874 to 1945) conducted 776 evangelistic campaigns and registered nearly three million decisions. He frequently spent two or three days fasting and praying and experienced the power of God on his ministry with souls responding, and then healings began to happen. One of the first cases was his own wife who had been suffering with a dangerous cancer on her neck for three years. After medical treatment at the mission hospital throughout that period had proved ineffective, they agreed to pray together for healing. Within two weeks she was completely healed.

Soon after this he got into discussion with another pastor about Mark 16:17–18 at a Bible conference week. He asked himself, why should God not give healing today if his power is still with us? He felt that it was because he had not asked in faith. It marked the start of a new era in his ministry.

A few weeks later he was leading a Bible conference in a village where there was a well-known case of a man who had suffered with a badly dislocated lower jaw for many years. The poor man lived as a beggar. Unable to eat properly and constantly dribbling at the mouth, he was a pathetic sight. Kim Ik-Du prayed for him. There was no change for two days and so on the third day Kim decided to fast. Some of the Christians said it was a hopeless case and there was no point in praying further. The next morning Kim was confronted with an excited crowd bringing the beggar, to show Kim that God had miraculously healed him. The beggar was able to eat and speak properly for the first time in ten years.

Soon Kim was praying for hundreds of sick people who flocked to his meetings. Many were healed, but doctors and church leaders united in their bitter opposition to this new ministry. Rather than be an instrument of dissension in the church, Kim Ik-Du ceased to give prominence to healing and though some healings still occurred his ministry to the sick diminished thereafter. He was martyred by the communists on 14th October 1950, just as he was pronouncing the benediction at the dawn prayer meeting. Soldiers burst in on them, shooting as they entered, and Kim Ik-Du fell fatally wounded and died within minutes.

From such a background of opposition to healing, it was obviously not going to be easy for anyone to bring healing to a place of wide acceptance in the churches of Korea. The fact that healing has become a vital part of the ministry in many of the churches of most denominations is due in no small measure to the ongoing ministry of Yonggi Cho. He has been a pacesetter in many areas of ministry and especially in this one. Nevertheless, it has not been easy for him. As he became known and started to preach outside Korea, to save confusion over his name he decided to add the Christian name of Paul to his Korean family name. Like Paul, though a chosen vessel God has allowed Yonggi Cho to suffer greatly, but out of the furnace of affliction he has come forth refined and a vessel unto honour.

Even a brief outline sketch of his ministry reveals a great deal of suffering. By 13th December 1964 the membership of his church at Sodaemoon had grown to around two thousand and they were able to open a new building. Three months later on 1st March 1965 he married Jashil Choi's gifted daughter Sung Hae Kim, who was a graduate of Ewha Women's University and a brilliant musician. Within a year their first child, a boy, was born, but their joy was short-lived when he was found to be suffering from asthma.

Although he was seeing a regular stream of healing miracles in the church, which were confirmed by doctors and of sufficient note to attract doctors to join his congregation, nothing happened when Yonggi Cho prayed for his own baby son. He and his young wife were driven to distraction by sleepless nights due to the baby's asthma attacks, and through seeing the little baby suffering so much. They quarrelled bitterly with each other; Cho prayed and prayed but to no effect. He even began to resent his son as an intrusion and a hindrance to his ministry. Then one day as the thought came to him afresh that this was his own flesh and blood and very dear to him just as Jesus was also unspeakably precious to the Father, he prayed again with a new love and compassion. The wheezing suddenly ceased; Yonggi Cho rushed to the cot afraid lest the baby had stopped breathing but he was sleeping peacefully for the first time in ages. They were delighted and relieved that the Lord Jesus had healed their son, but they were still mystified as to how and why it had happened. All these events blended together to ensure a balanced approach to divine healing.

Yonggi Cho knows there are mysteries to healing and that God is sovereign in these matters. But he also knows that prayer, prevailing prayer, constant prayer, is the key to an ongoing and ever-increasing ministry in this, just as it is in soul-winning. At the Annual Women's Conference at Prayer Mountain in 1987, just a few weeks before our arrival in Korea, some 10,000 people gathered. Yonggi Cho preached and then prayed for God's kingdom to come with power for healing right there. As he prayed five women got up out of their wheelchairs and walked.

However, Yonggi Cho is not a fanatic. Every week he now schedules his amazingly busy life to include two rounds of golf. Conscious of his need to take exercise and look after his health (which was restored only after ten years of constant prayer), he tried jogging. But one morning while out jogging in France where he was conducting a crusade, he collapsed on the pavement, gasping for breath and in a distressed state. He was told by a doctor never to jog again as it was too much for his heart. Instead he should play golf because on the golf course one walks. Yonggi Cho complained that golf takes up too much time and he was too busy and did not have time to spare. The doctor asked him to think again. Knowing that he had been healed of tuberculosis, the doctor told him that the space of his heart was restricted and consequently it had to pump blood three times faster than normal. Cholesterol was also building up in his blood vessels and so exercise was imperative. He advised Yonggi Cho that regular exercise would lengthen his life by ten years or more.

Conversation with one of his senior ministers revealed that Cho has become quite a good golfer and enjoys it.

As with everything else, he takes it quite seriously and likes to win. Mostly he plays with some of his close colleagues and makes it a time to enjoy fellowship on a very relaxed level. I also gathered that their ambition is to beat him, and there is never any thought of deliberately letting him win!

It should be made clear that the healing ministry in Yoido Full Gospel Church is by no means confined to Yonggi Cho. Because of the size of the congregation, the use of spiritual gifts in the main services is understandably confined to the platform; but all are encouraged to use spiritual gifts in the house cells. When miracles of healing occur in the small groups they make maximum impact in the immediate locality. For example, around the time we were there they had been especially praying in one of the local districts for three couples who had each been married for several years without producing any children. The couples had all visited the hospital but were still barren. The cell leaders and those directly involved took these couples on their hearts and began to pray that God would bless these marriages and make them fruitful for his glory. Imagine the joy and thanksgiving when in due time all three couples reported that babies had been conceived.

At every level these Christians expect miracles to happen when they pray, and from time to time God grants them outstanding signs and wonders which raise their faith to ever greater heights. Yonggi Cho's personal secretary, Mrs Lydia Swain, told us of several such incidents, one of which really thrilled the whole church when it became known. Three years ago there was serious flooding which was threatening Yoido Island; it had been raining ceaselessly for several weeks and the River Han had risen almost to the level of the roads on the great bridges linking the island with the rest of Seoul. The situation was serious and the Christians set themselves to pray for the rains to cease. Their prayers were answered and the rains stopped but many of the roads and streets were still under water.

A family of new Christians, just recently converted, had joined one of the house cells. Their little boy aged seven was walking home from school with another friend, and as boys will do they were walking in the middle of the street and kicking up the water as they went. It just so happened that right in their path was an unmarked manhole, and probably because of the storms its cover was missing. Suddenly the little seven-year-old boy fell through it and disappeared from view. The other boy was panic stricken: what had happened? What could he do? Then he remembered that they were near the cell leader's house and so he ran as fast as his little legs would carry him. It so happened that this boy's family belonged to the same house cell. Fortunately the cell leader was at home—a woman of prayer. He poured out his tale of woe, pleading with her,

'Come quickly, come quickly, my friend has fallen in . . . let's pray . . .'

The cell leader dropped everything and ran with him back to the place. She stood by the manhole and prayed for an hour-and-a-half. Passers-by came over to see what she was doing, and when they learned what had happened they all said,

'Woman, you are crazy, he's already been swept out to the ocean and he's gone. Forget it,' and they walked away; but she ignored them and continued praying and asking God for a miracle.

When at last the waters had subsided to a level where they were able to get down into the manhole, to their amazement they discovered the little boy crouching there with his face between his knees and his hands in a position as though he were gripping something. When they pulled him out they found he was still alive and when they had revived him he told them,

'Just as I was falling in a tall man dressed in white

stood by me and said, "Grab the rope and hold on," so I did.' He thought that he was still holding the rope but of course there was no visible rope.

Our materialistic Western brand of Christianity finds that kind of thing very hard to accept, but Korean believers are persuaded in their own minds that just as in the days of the apostles, 'the Lord hath sent his angel, and hath delivered him' (Acts 12:11) — so it still happens. I have a feeling the apostle Peter would not have had any difficulty believing that story. I also have a very strong idea that the early church would have more readily identified themselves with that kind of praying than with our passive Western brand. After all, did not a whole crowd of them 'pray without ceasing' for Peter's escape from prison and execution (Acts 12:5)?

There are those, of course, who attribute this whole area of angels and demons to the Korean background of Shamanism and treat it with great suspicion. It is a fact that religiously Koreans are more influenced by Shamanism (folk religion) or animism than by an organised religion like Buddhism. Shamanism is thought to be the original religion of Korea and is closely akin to spiritism. Through the centuries this ancient religion continually added to the vast number of gods, demons and demigods. There were spirits of disease, spirits of the mountain passes, spirits in trees and rocks, spirits everywhere and in almost everything. They demanded to be placated or warded off, and so there developed a correspondingly great number of fetishes and charms. There also arose those who claimed to have the power to drive out spirits which were troubling people, for a fee of course. Women specialising in this became known as 'mudangs'. Fortune-tellers also flourished, and the ones who contrived to make this their special field of operation were blind men, known as 'pansoons'. Such a religion of superstition is based on fear, with the result that the average Korean was more concerned with relief from trouble and with personal

benefits than with moral values. It seems that Koreans
have always had a deep-rooted conviction of the presence
of spiritual beings.

Reliable Korean church historians such as Lak-Geoon
George Paik give it as their considered opinion that the
mass of the people opted for the best of all worlds and in
effect combined the main features of their three ancient
religions of Shamanism, Buddhism and Confucianisim.
'As a result,' says Paik, 'the average Korean takes his
religious ceremonies from ancestor worship, seeks the
efficacy of Buddhistic prayers, devoutly bows his head at
the shrine of the mountain demons, and recites Confucian
classics.' However, his summing up of the situation is very
important and instructive: 'On the surface, the religious
syncretism of the Korean people may seem an indication
of a total indifference and undue tolerance toward religion,
but examined more closely it shows a religious hunger.'

That deep religious hunger has found satisfaction at
last in Christianity. Koreans readily identify with the
Gospels as they read about demons, but the attraction in
this case is that the demons are on the run: in Jesus they
have at last found one who has power over all demons
and who offers peace to those who trust him. The average
Westerner is suffering such massive overdoses of human-
istic fall-out that he or she cannot believe anything that
smacks even remotely of the supernatural. There is a
danger that the average Korean might now be at the
opposite end of the scale and ready to believe everything.
Fortunately the Korean Christian leaders are alert to this
and counter it from the very first moment of decision.
The singing of the Lord's Prayer and the reciting of the
Apostles' Creed in every service is a deliberate ploy. The
Ten Commandments are also brought into regular use.
Immediately a person makes a profession of salvation they
are faced with the first commandment: 'Thou shalt have
no other gods before me.' It is made clear with a firmness
which is admirable that total commitment to the Lord

is the first requisite of being a Christian. Anything and everything relating to other religions, other gods, familiar spirits and the like, must be renounced.

Once cleansed and set free, it does seem that Koreans have a wonderful capacity for faith. The growing ministry of healing in the church in Korea is by no means confined to Yonggi Cho's church. His influence has been tremendous but across the city at the world's biggest Methodist church, Kwang Lim Church, the godly minister the Revd Dr Kim Sun-Do regards divine healing as a vital part of his work. As he was a fully qualified medical doctor, a graduate of Haeju Medical College, before entering the Methodist ministry, this adds credence to healings which occur in his church. His aim is to make Kwang Lim a healing centre for those who have lost the meaning of life and are hurting and bruised by modern society.

To sit in the services at Kwang Lim and listen to Dr Kim Sun-Do preach is a tremendous experience. His preaching is anointed and positive and is meeting with a tremendous response. Every week people are coming to Christ and being added to his church. He is an anointed servant of God who has experienced a definite infilling of the Holy Spirit and who believes in and regularly exercises the gifts of the Spirit. He prays for the sick and believes in laying his hands upon them when the situation warrants it and it is convenient.

He told me that when he felt the burden to extend his church and build a great new sanctuary in 1978, he set himself aside to seek the face of God and he prayed and fasted for twenty days. That is the great secret behind this faith-inspiring church. When they started to build they had no money and the total cost was some four million American dollars. It was a great venture of faith; but God met their needs, the money came in, and this superlative structure stands as further evidence of positive Korean faith and love. Dr Kim Sun-Do is a truly humble servant of Jesus Christ, and his church is a tangible token of effective evangelistic outreach which is being confirmed by signs and wonders. His church, and others like it, are living and undeniable proof that far from diminishing, the revival is still burning brightly in Korea, and the stream of miracles is a growing part of it.

10

The Miracle of Prayer Mountains

The Korean peninsula is one of the world's most moun-
tainous regions, with only a fifth of it flat and suitable for
cultivation. A north–south chain of mountains forms an
impressive backbone down the centre of the country. The
Korean Christians have put many of these barren hills to
good use—they have made them into prayer mountains.
Dotted all over South Korea are dozens of such places
which have been purchased by various churches for use
as prayer retreats. They have become a regular feature of
Korean church life as places where Christians can set
themselves to seek God in prayer and fasting.

Fasting has long been regarded as an indispensable
part of prayer by keen Korean Christians. In 1980 as
part of Korea's World Evangelisation Crusade, the many
churches involved organised a forty-day national prayer
and fasting campaign. It was a call to the then seven
million Christians of Korea to seek God for a nationwide
spiritual awakening. Every Christian was urged to fast
from at least one meal per week throughout the forty days.
A special feature was a three-day prayer and fasting rally
at the Hanul Mountain Prayer Retreat Centre. More than
30,000 turned up for this but 10,000 had to be sent away
for lack of room. It took place at the end of February and
the weather was cold. The building could only hold 10,000
so they divided into two groups and changed places every

two hours; 10,000 prayed inside while the other 10,000 prayed on the mountainside in the bitter cold. Throughout the long build-up to the crusade, groups of 300 students rotated daily for a period of seventeen months to keep the fires of fasting and prayer burning. No wonder God blessed in a remarkable way, with thousands coming to Christ and many thousands of Christians committing themselves to volunteer for missionary service.

Dr Kim Sun-Do told us that his Kwang Lim Methodist Church had recently acquired their own prayer mountain to use for regular prayer retreats, and as a place where Christians could go to pray and fast for a day, a week, or even a month. A chain of fasting prayer had been organised between various members of his church and was in progress at the time we were with him. The famous Young Nak Presbyterian Church also has a prayer centre on the northern side of the city which is used by many of the members. Indeed, Korean leaders will tell you that every deep mountain valley now has prayer houses where men and women pray and fast, sometimes for as long as forty days. They believe that this is one of the reasons why they enjoy so much of the presence and power of God in their churches.

Almost inevitably it seems, the biggest and most-used prayer mountain is the one belonging to Yoido Full Gospel Church. A visit to Prayer Mountain was one of the things we had been looking forward to most of all. As it happened we made three visits, including the very special privilege of spending time with Dr Jashil Choi in her home on Prayer Mountain.

Buses depart for Prayer Mountain at hourly intervals throughout the day from the side of the World Mission Centre. This shuttle service is free. They never leave empty and mostly they are filled to capacity with a wide variety of people of all ages bent on one thing: seeking God. Mothers take their babies and young children. There is never the problem of getting prams or pushchairs on the bus—Korean mothers never use such contraptions. With an adroitness acquired through many generations, Korean mothers carry their children on their backs. The babies snuggle contentedly there in a simple sling skilfully made out of a large shawl, which is always at hand to serve as a blanket or sheet to cover the babies when the opportunity comes to lay them down somewhere. Korean mothers seem not to bother about babysitters; they take their babies everywhere with them.

It is an experience in itself to watch the people loading on to the buses. Some are travelling light and probably just going up for the day; others have obviously come equipped to spend several days there. They carry their rolled-up blankets and other such basic necessities of life. Some look ill and they probably are, because it is a regular thing for sick people to go to Prayer Mountain to pray and fast for a week or ten days to seek healing from God. Many go who have cancer: Christ is their last and only hope. Not all are healed, but a great number of such cases claim healing. One recent figure claimed that over 70 per cent of those attending this prayer mountain were healed.

When the bus is ready to leave, the driver signals that it is time for some brief devotions, which come in the form of a taped prayer followed by music relayed over the bus audio system. But there is nothing mechanical about the reaction of the people on the crowded bus; they respond readily and warmly with their usual amens and hallelujahs. The bus is quite spartan—nothing luxurious—just the kind of ordinary vehicle which serves most local bus routes in Britain. Gospel music plays throughout the journey, which lasts about an hour and is a little less than thirty miles. The route lies through the centre of Seoul and out on one of the main highways to the north. A few miles out of the city the bus has to slow down to pass through a checkpoint which is manned by police and military. This is quite normal for Korea. The buses from Yoido Full Gospel Church are well known and so there is seldom any problem. However, those who stay the night at Prayer Mountain and want to leave before dawn have to remember that a curfew still operates and this check-point is shut until 4 am.

Once clear of the city, the countryside is unusual and interesting. There are paddy fields on either side and peasants can be seen working in them in the time-honoured manner. Men and women work up to their knees in water, tending the rice which still forms a large part of their diet. The scenery is fascinating and some of it beautiful, but potholes abound in the road and the ride is by no means smooth. The quite large number of soldiers (American and Korean) marching in single file along the side of the road, engaged in a military exercise, is a salu-tary reminder that South Korea lives in a state of constant tension with communist North Korea.

After a few more miles the bus turns off the main road at the place where a sign proclaims: 'Yoido Full Gospel Church: International Prayer Mountain'. The countryside at Osanri in the Kyunggi province is beautiful and at its summer best. But the regular sound of gunfire is another reminder that just a few miles on the other side of this small mountain lies the infamous DMZ (Demilitarised Zone) and the 38th parallel which now divides this ancient nation in two. The church owns land over on the other side of the mountain, still in South Korea, but at present it is being used by South Korean troops for training and for firing practice. It is a relief to be assured that the gunfire is only target practice. Nevertheless it is mildly disturbing to find young, baby-faced (and dirty-faced) Korean soldiers constantly popping up all around the coach parking area. There is no denying that such happenings do stimulate prayer.

It is amazing to find how much the church has developed the site, which covers some sixty acres. As people pile out of the bus there is a security guard on duty at the gate checking everyone who enters. Everything is friendly but efficient. Everyone has to register. Some who want to stay for several days have already booked special rooms which are available with bunk beds and showers. This particular week is a special time of prayer for the nation because it is when they remember the treacherous invasion by North Korea on the Sunday morning of 25th June 1950 which signalled the beginning of the Korean War.

The first thing that strikes one is the number of buses and coaches here—well over a hundred of them, all parked in long lines. Many of them belong to just one of the districts, whole coachloads of people out for a special day of prayer. They are accommodated in one of the smaller buildings where some 1,500 of them are to be found sitting cross-legged on the floor, Korean fashion. The district pastor and his team are leading the session and one of them is just finishing preaching. Soon they are all singing one of the old, well-known gospel hymns, in Korean of course, with the familiar tune but with unfamiliar fervour and tremendous clapping. Such treatment ensures that these hymns take on new life. When they start praying, all 1,500 of them, it is rather like one of the great old steam trains getting under way and moving along with terrifying power and thundering noise. Yet, just as in the church, the same orderliness prevails here, and the ringing of a little bell by the senior minister brings the 'fifteen-hundred-men-and-women-powered prayer train' to a halt just when and where the driver wants it!

The main sanctuary is quite new and very imaginative and modern. It is built in the form of a great Noah's ark, and is capable of holding up to 10,000 people (Korean style, of course). Inside, the scene is impressive. The huge building is well filled and another Korean pastor is leading the devotions. In the area immediately in front of the platform hundreds of people are squatting on their blankets and bedrolls. Many of them also have their bottles of water and clearly most of them have come to fast as

well as pray. Hundreds more are sitting in the scores of
wooden pews which form a huge semicircle around the
platform. At the back of the auditorium several people
are stretched out on the floor on their mats, fast asleep.
Koreans can squat and sleep anywhere. Many of these
people have given up a week of their holidays to spend
the time praying and fasting.

Not all have come seeking healing. Professor Marlin
Nelson shared with me that, according to one of his
students who was doing research about Prayer Mountain,
more come seeking to be filled with the Holy Spirit than
for healing. This confirms the claim of the church that
most people come to Prayer Mountain seeking the
baptism of the Holy Spirit. No quick laying on of hands
and 'now speak in tongues' for these people—they have
come meaning business with God and they are prepared
to wait on God for a mighty infilling of the Holy Spirit.
Others have come to pray about church problems; or
about family matters, especially for their unsaved relatives; some have come with personal and business problems, believing that prayer is the answer to every situation; and divine healing is last on the list. It is also
illuminating to discover that of the 3,000 lay believers
who visit Prayer Mountain daily, records reveal that 42
per cent are Presbyterian, 16.5 per cent Methodist, 13.2
per cent Holiness, 13 per cent Full Gospel and 5.6 per
cent Baptist.

Koreans can squat anywhere but Westerners don't find
it so easy, especially when sessions last for several hours.
One American student, over from Oral Roberts University studying Korean church growth, was up at Prayer
Mountain with the district group to which he was
assigned. He found himself sitting cross-legged on the
floor, jammed in the middle of hundreds of Koreans.
There was the usual preaching and praying and all was
going well until he got cramp. He endured the agony
thinking the session would soon be over, but it went on

for four hours. By the time it finished he could not move—
they had to lift him up and massage his legs and feet for
a considerable time before he got relief!

The site of Prayer Mountain was a cemetery before the
church bought it; in fact it was originally purchased for
use as the church's own cemetery. But Dr Jashil Choi,
Yonggi Cho's mother-in-law, had other ideas. Once she
had seen it she laid claim to it for a prayer mountain.
The cemetery is still maintained, but there are now trees
and many flowers and shrubs beautifying the whole area.
Behind the main sanctuary the little prayer grottos are
dotted in splendid profusion under the trees on the
hillside.

Many Westerners arrive here cherishing romantic
notions about praying like a Finney or a Brainerd in one
of the grottos, but the cold, stark reality of these small,
one-person concrete caves quickly dispels all fantasies.
150 of these are built on the mountainside. There is a
door and ventilation grill but little else, and they are not
large enough to allow one to stand upright. Once inside
with the door shut, it is dark unless you have brought
your own candle, and it is a matter of kneel, crouch or
curl up—no room to stretch up or stretch out. But the
numbers of pairs of shoes outside these grottos and the
sound of fervent praying issuing from within, indicate that
they are almost all occupied. Clearly the Koreans find
them acceptable. Many shut themselves in and pray and
fast for days and nights, with their blankets wrapped
around them. Yonggi Cho's private grotto is equally
spartan. He has spent countless hours here seeking God—
especially in times of crisis. He is frequently here on
Saturday afternoons, to prepare himself for the Sunday
services by waiting on the Lord.

The splendid new dormitory block is somewhat in
contrast to the prayer grottos, with excellent bedrooms,
showers and toilet facilities, as well as dormitories for
groups who wish to stay together. It is still not luxurious

but it indicates the ever-growing numbers coming to Prayer Mountain, and it is an attempt to especially cater for the increasing number of businessmen and women from Japan and other parts of the world who are beginning to find their way to Prayer Mountain.

In all it is now claimed that 20,000 people can worship here in the main sanctuary, the two other chapels, and the seven smaller chapels. There is overnight accommodation for 3,000 at a nominal charge. The whole project is staggering in its immensity as well as in its intensity. There is a large permanent staff to see that everything runs smoothly in the area of the natural as well as the spiritual. Twenty full-time pastors serve here, and between them they organise four services daily. They also arrange seminars, and students come here for a prayer and fasting camp every summer. The different districts also come out here on a regular basis for a day, or a day and a night, of prayer.

In many ways it is very different from what is generally imagined. For one thing, it is far more organised. A great deal of the praying is co-ordinated from the platform, and there is more preaching and singing than people usually anticipate. It is also not unknown for other Christian leaders to criticise, as well as unsaved husbands or wives. They complain that people are spending too much time praying at Prayer Mountain and neglecting their families. I can only say that I am sure most ministers of my acquaintance in the West would welcome the opportunity to have to deal with such criticism.

One thing is certain: there is a tremendous lot of praying done by an amazing number of people, and there are wonderful answers to prayer all the time at the International Prayer Mountain. Jashil Choi is praying that one day there will be a prayer mountain in Britain. I am sure that many intercessors will breathe a fervent 'Amen' to that request.

I I

The Miracle of the Woman Behind the Mountain

A day of days for us was when we met the person responsible for founding International Prayer Mountain, Dr Jashil Choi. Mrs Swain kindly made the appointment for us as Dr Choi speaks very little English and our Korean is nil. Mrs Swain also very kindly loaned us one of her secretaries, Miss Lee, to act as our interpreter, as well as putting her car and driver at our disposal. The day we met this outstanding woman of prayer was perfect in every way; a day which will remain with both my wife and myself for the rest of our lives. In many ways this was predominantly my wife Hazel's day. Because she is involved with various groups of women intercessors in England, she had specially asked for this interview. There was an immediate rapport between Hazel and Jashil and for the most part I felt myself to be just a privileged spectator. Whatever our views about women's ministry, there is no doubt that when it comes to praying the women are in front of the men.

The weather was idyllic, with warm sunshine and a few fleecy clouds adorning a blue sky, as we made a much faster and more comfortable trip out to Prayer Mountain than the one on the church bus. Dr Jashil Choi's home is just off a side road leading up to the main sanctuary. It is a modest Korean house; clean, compact, pleasantly furnished but devoid of any luxury—her simple lifestyle fits in with the image of a woman of prayer. There was a time in her life when she was wealthy and material things dominated, but no longer; now the spiritual comes first.

Dr Jashil Choi came out of the house to greet us in the very warmest manner, and immediately we were set at ease and felt truly welcome. We had deliberately done without our breakfast, expecting that this would be a day of fasting, but we quickly discovered otherwise. We removed our shoes at the door and entered to find that breakfast was already prepared for us. By now we were getting somewhat accustomed to Korean ways and we squatted down on the beautiful satin cushions set out around the low dining table on the polished wood floor. We soon found that Jashil is an expert in health foods as well as on fasting, and everything we drank was natural and devoid of any harmful chemicals.

Having watched her earlier from afar, when she was sharing the platform with Yonggi Cho and praying at the ordination of elders and deacons, we had already formed an impression of her. On the platform she was clearly enjoying the service and was 'very free in the spirit', to use a charismatic expression. She lifted her hands in worship; clapped in ecstasy at moments of joy; prayed in the most vigorous and attractive manner when laying hands on individual elders at ordination. Not content with laying on hands she also patted them rapidly as she spoke to them words of encouragement and exhortation, intent on making sure that she imparted a spiritual blessing to them, even if she had to tap it into them! We had formed the impression that she was a 'woman of spiritual substance', a strong personality, dominant, who would stand no nonsense; yet at the same time all these qualities which could so easily prove forbidding were offset by a wonderful jolliness that indicated a strong love of life.

Close up, we found that our first impressions were quite accurate. She is small in stature but pleasantly plumpish—for all her fasting. Her round face is lit up by her bright eyes, which we found searching us and sizing us up. She has a kind housekeeper who was very busy in the kitchen attending to our wants. It was soon clear who was in charge: Dr Jashil Choi! Firmly but kindly she gave the orders, which were carried out immediately and to the letter.

Hazel drew out of her the story behind International Prayer Mountain, as well as her own thrilling story. Sitting opposite this vivacious woman it was hard to believe that she is seventy-two years of age and that she has endured more than her fair share of suffering and hardship. She met with much antagonism before she started Prayer Mountain in the early 1970s. She came up to the site and prayed every night for 100 days before the project went ahead. She poured out her very soul, weeping and praying night after night. She fasted for ten days and then ate a little and asked God to show her a sign if this was the place. She prayed for ninety days and still there was no sign from God. Then on the ninety-first day a 26-year-old man who was dying from tuberculosis came and asked her to bring him to the mountain, even if he was going to die. She was a midwife and a nurse before entering the ministry and she remembered that the tuberculosis bacteria die in five days in the sun. She told him to fast and pray for five days. After five days he was somewhat improved and so she asked him if he wanted to end his fast. He said he wanted to continue fasting for another five days, by which time he was healed. She arranged for him to be sent to a seminary to train for the ministry. After completing his training he pioneered a church some distance from Seoul and God blessed his ministry with many healings and souls. This was the sign Jashil Choi had been looking for.

Prayer Mountain started very simply, without buildings and facilities, but she and others came to pray and fast. In fact she herself came to the mountain to pray every night for three years. They made do with a tent until the first sanctuary was opened on 30th July 1974. For over ten years there has not been a single day without a service at Prayer Mountain.

Prayer requests come here from all over the world as well as from all over Korea; to date, letters asking for special prayer have been received from 108 different countries. When the letters arrive at Yoido, Mrs Swain reads them first and then summarises the requests for Yonggi Cho, who prays for them himself before sending the letters up to intercessors at Prayer Mountain, who take the burdens on their hearts and pray at length for them. Prayer is taken very seriously, and only eternity will reveal all the miracles which have happened around the world because of Prayer Mountain and the faith of this little woman who founded it.

Jashil Choi was born on 15th August 1915 in the northern part of Korea in the Pyongyang area. (Korea was still one country in those days, but as we have seen, it was very much a police state under Japanese domination.) Her father died when she was only five years old. He was one of the many zealous Korean patriots who refused to accept Japanese rule. Often he was away from home for months at a time supporting a Korean independence movement over the border in China. Following the open Declaration of Independence in 1919 which had been supported by millions of Koreans, the Japanese had reacted savagely. Zealots like Jashil's father were ruthlessly sought out. When he fell into their cruel hands he was tortured to extract information, until finally, battered, with some of his teeth knocked out, bruised and dying, he was moved to an hospital in Pyongyang. His wife hurried to his bedside with Jashil and her baby brother; it was the last time they saw him—he died that night.

Jashil grew up and went to school in the little village of Haeju, located to the south-east of the Sooyang Mountains. Life under the Japanese was doubly hard for one-parent families, but her mother bravely coped in the little wood-framed, mud-coated house, thatched with rice straw and lit by a solitary oil lamp. Food was scarce and Jashil grew up with hunger as a familiar and unwelcome companion.

In spite of everything the Japanese did, the churches continued to thrive, and none more so than those in Pyongyang where Jashil lived as a teenager. In 1928 another wave of revival swept through the growing town. Evangelism was the order of the day, with fruitful crusades in tents and school halls. The erection of a big tent was an event in those days, and when one was put up beside the church near her home, Jashil readily agreed to a friend's invitation to go along. The tent was already full when they arrived, with people standing, but they crawled under the edge of the tent and Jashil found herself squatting on the floor right in front of the pulpit. The evangelist was called Lee Song Bong and he was another who not only preached the gospel faithfully but who also believed in praying for the sick. His preaching answered many of the questions which had been troubling Jashil's young head for a long time, but when he prayed for a woman neighbour who was afflicted with a deformed and twisted arm and Jashil saw her stretch it out and wave it in the air, she was convinced.

Jashil simply could not wait. At the first opportunity, as the people were singing and clapping and rejoicing at what God was doing in the tent, she slipped out and ran home to fetch her mother who suffered with migraine headaches. Jesus could surely heal her, too. She poured out her story to her mother, already pulling at her arm to persuade her to come down to the tent immediately. But instead of being pleased, her mother was angry; she was a Buddhist and did not want any of this Jesus business. Jashil started to cry, and she cried so much that her mother said she would go and see what it was all about just to placate her. At the tent mother and daughter both crawled under the edge of the canvas, and for the first time her mother heard something of the gospel as the evangelist continued to exhort people to repent before praying for them. She joined the line of those waiting for healing. Lee Song Bong prayed for her, and that was the last of her migraines and the beginning of her new life as a Christian. From then on it seemed to Jashil that her mother was always praying, and often she did so in a new language that Jashil could not understand.

Life was different after that. Gradually things improved, and Jashil's mother made rapid progress in her Christian life. Eventually she became the head deaconess in the Second Presbyterian Church in Pyongyang. She frequently spent whole nights praying and weeping before the Lord, and Jashil grew up in an atmosphere of prayer and of constant exhortation to seek first the kingdom of God and all the necessities of life would be added unto her. It worked, too. At eighteen years of age Jashil was one of only five Koreans accepted for training as a nurse, out of hundreds of applicants. She successfully completed her two-year course, then went on to qualify as a midwife. To gain more money, she volunteered to serve in the dangerous northern border area where Manchurian bandits frequently raided, murdering and plundering the villages.

Money became important to her and her priorities subtly changed. In time she found herself in a position to establish her own clinic in Pyongyang. Soon she was becoming quite well off, but to her mother's dismay and disgust Jashil began to open her clinic on Sundays to make more money. Next she met and fell in love with a handsome young naval officer, Chang Ki Kim, and they were married on 29th April 1940. She had three babies in fairly quick succession, but still contrived to keep the clinic going.

The Japanese were finally defeated and the war ended on 15th August 1945, the day of Jashil's thirtieth birthday. Celebrations were short-lived on both counts. Within two weeks they found the cruel Japanese were replaced by the ruthless Russians and their country cut in two by the 38th parallel. News leaked out that their new taskmasters intended deporting to Siberia all Korean government officials who had worked with the Japanese; Jashil's husband came in that category and so he and Jashil's brother made immediate plans to escape to the south of the country where the Americans were in control. Jashil was left with her three young children and her mother to face life under the communists.

At first all seemed well. Pastors and many Christians were released from prison; other Christian leaders and believers came out into the open after being virtually an 'underground church' for the last dreadful years of oppression under the Japanese. But within a matter of months they began to discover the unacceptable face of North Korean communism. Headed by Kim Il-Sung the communists mercilessly set about their goal of establishing a restrictive, totalitarian state. Churches were burned; pastors who resisted were killed; the long-cherished hopes of freedom vanished.

Jashil determined to flee to South Korea, hoping there to find that her husband's bid for freedom had been successful. Along with her mother and three young children (all no more than babies), she made her attempt in March 1946. They left their home for the border, where they discovered a man willing to undertake the risky business of guiding them across—for a price, of course. Waiting for the cover of a dark, rainy night, for which they prayed earnestly, they set off on their perilous adventure. The children and grandmother were hidden in the guide's ox cart, while Jashil walked behind and the guide led the oxen. Russians with dogs constantly patrolled the zone, but thanks to a welcome mist as well as the rain, their prayers were answered. Although they had a few very anxious moments, the guide at last assured them that they were across the border.

Their troubles were not over yet, however. Before they had gone very far, looters, who waited for hapless refugees from North Korea in the knowledge that they carried their life savings with them, tried to hold them up. Thanks to fervent prayer and quick thinking by Jashil, who pretended they were armed and had men hidden in the wagon, the looters fled.

Jashil was reunited with her husband in Seoul and very soon she was using her many abilities and business acumen to make money. First she established a maternity clinic, then she extended into other ventures such as making soap and matches, as well as opening another clinic—not to mention producing another baby, a boy. Then just when everything seemed to be going so well for her, with the prestige of serving on some high government committees as well as her growing wealth, the communists invaded and the Korean War started on 25th June 1950. Once again Jashil gathered her children and her belongings and fled for her life. They stayed in hiding in the mountains for months as the fighting went to and fro. Eventually she was able to rejoin her husband in Chinhae, and in a short time she was involved in another business, this time as the owner of a small factory producing spindles. Once again she began to prosper and soon was able to run a chauffeur-driven car, but she was now thoroughly backslidden and neglected both the family of God and her own family in her quest for riches.

Her mother prayed for her and constantly warned her. Then a double tragedy struck: Jashil's eldest daughter, Bokja, aged sixteen years, was knocked down by a car and had to be taken to hospital; on top of this Jashil's mother took ill and died. Less than two weeks after burying her mother, a shattered and broken Jashil found herself at the funeral of her daughter also. Things continued to go wrong, and Jashil found her world collapsing around her when the Korean currency was devalued, resulting in her bankruptcy. She was utterly devastated and decided that suicide was the only way out. Determining to fast to death, she arranged for relatives to care for her three remaining children.

En route to the mountains where she intended to carry through her plan to fast to death, Jashil stopped for one final meal. There, in the providence of God, for the first time in twenty years she met an old friend who had also fled from North Korea. Unaware of Jashil's intentions, she invited her to a special evangelistic crusade which was in progress. Jashil refused, but her friend persisted and insisted until Jashil yielded. In the meeting she found an enthusiastic crowd of about 1,000 singing and clapping. She was not impressed. The preacher was an old man with white hair, and it was only when he stood up and started to preach that she recognised him—it was Lee Song Bong, the evangelist she had first heard in the tent as a girl, thirty years before. His message had hardly changed; the words went straight to her heart and she could not resist the Spirit of God any longer. Broken and tearful she confessed her sins and asked the Lord for his forgiveness. It was not a superficial confession; she let the Holy Spirit search and probe until every sin was confessed and put away.

Restored and renewed, Jashil felt she should devote herself to the work of the Lord and asked the Revd Lee Song Bong for his advice about her entering the Presbyterian Bible College. He directed her to a Bible school in Seoul which had been opened only two or three years. It was the Full Gospel Bible Institute, which was under the auspices of the American Assemblies of God. The guidance was surely from God, for it was there that the renewed Jashil Choi met a raw young Korean student called Yonggi Cho.

Jashil was forty-one years old when she entered the Full Gospel Bible Institute in 1956, and Yonggi Cho just twenty. The restored Jashil was too much for most people to take; now she was always praying. Her husband had a weakness for the ladies and he suddenly left her to live with a much younger woman. She had to endure a lot of persecution; even some of the students were unkind. She was called 'Hallelujah Woman' and 'Crazy Mother'. People said,

'She can't help it, she is over forty years old and crazy because her husband has left her for another woman, and on top of that she doesn't eat anything.'

There was also a certain amount of jealousy because 'Hallelujah Woman' was rich enough to have her own car and a chauffeur, and she could afford the very best clothes. Unlike the other students who lived in the barest of dormitories, she had her home and travelled in each day in style. She was also the most zealous student in the place.

Jashil prayed for her husband for ten years. In addition to being very handsome he was a clever man; well educated, he was a graduate of Tokyo University. Even when he divorced her she continued to pray for him. He took a second woman and still she prayed. After ten years he could hold out against her prayers no longer. He repented and was restored both to her and to the Lord. He began to work for the Lord, and assisted his son-in-law Yonggi Cho as well as undertaking missionary work in Japan because of his fluency in the Japanese language. He was faithful to the Lord and to Jashil until his death.

After hearing her story and talking with her about prayer, she took us up to the main sanctuary at Prayer Mountain. When Jashil Choi is around everyone jumps to attention, and it was intriguing to see the affection and esteem in which she is held by everyone. After sharing in the meeting she took us on a grand tour of Prayer Mountain before taking us back to her home, where she insisted on our staying for lunch. Miss Lee was anxious to return to the office where a pile of work awaited her, but once again it was a fascinating experience to watch the clash of wills. There was never any doubt as to who was going to win. I pity the man, or woman, or demon, who dares to take on this redoubtable woman.

There is only one letter of difference between fast and feast. Lunch we quickly discovered was a feast, a Korean feast, specially prepared in our honour. Jashil had had her helpers working all morning to prepare us a sample of just about every Korean dish imaginable. The Korean custom is not to talk very much over a meal; eating is important business and should not be interrupted by too much talk. Koreans also tend to eat rapidly, and being inexpert with chopsticks does not help when the various dishes are brought to the table in a seemingly endless and rapid procession. Jashil was quick to tell us about the various dishes, especially the famous Korean Kimch'i. This is made from Chinese cabbage, and is highly seasoned with red pepper and garlic; the cabbage had been grown in her own little garden and no chemical fertilisers used, only organic. The taste is hot—very hot. We were given lots of the equally famous Korean drink of ginseng, which is claimed to be 'the panacea for all diseases which require the temperature to be raised', and is said to 'check senility, give vitality to the feeble, and step up digestion'. By the end of the fabulous feast we were in a position to put that claim to the test! Jashil informed us that she had recently had a check-up by her doctor, and his verdict is that she has the body of a forty-year-old and is in prime health. For this she gives God the glory, but she does believe that fasting and wise eating play a part.

The meal over, a worried Miss Lee finally ushered us back to the car; she was anxious to get back to the office. Koreans are reputed to be among the hardest workers in the world—and in the church offices they expect as much and even more from their staff as any secular business house. That evening Jashil was taking an evangelistic and healing crusade at the Sodaemoon church (Yonggi Cho's second church). We were looking forward to seeing her in action in her role as an evangelist with a healing and deliverance ministry. Unfortunately the student demonstrations and riot police tear gas prevented us from attending. In the morning we were not in the least surprised to learn that Jashil Choi had got through—it takes more than a riot to stop this amazing woman of God.

'The effectual fervent prayer of a righteous man availeth much' (Jas 5:16b), and Jashil Choi is living proof that the effectual fervent prayer of a righteous woman avails just as much. Her prayers have not only moved mountains they have built Prayer Mountain, which has also been the inspiration for pastors from America and Europe to establish their own prayer mountains.

The story is told of a church which was looking to fill their vacant pastorate. Seeking help from the area superintendent, he asked them what kind of a man they were looking for: were they hoping to attract a well-known minister, in other words were they wanting 'a big man'?

'No,' replied the church secretary, 'we are just looking for a man who is big enough to touch heaven when he is on his knees.' In Jashil Choi, Hazel and I knew that we had found a woman who had succeeded in building a prayer mountain where thousands of ordinary believers have discovered that they are big enough in Christ to reach heaven when they are on their knees.

I2

The Miracle of Growth by Cells

A rose by any other name would smell as sweet, and a house cell by any other name is just as effective. John Wesley is credited with being not only the founder of Methodism but also the instigator of the Wesleyan Class Meeting—and what is a house cell but a class meeting under another name?

There is a charming story that when the first Methodist missionaries, the Revd and Mrs Henry Appenzeller, and the Presbyterian Missionary the Revd Horace Underwood arrived at Inchon on Easter morning 5th April 1885, they joined hands and jumped ashore together so that posterity would not be able to claim that either denomination had arrived first. Unfortunately, like many good stories, it does not seem to be substantiated by fact. The truth appears to be that, being Christian gentlemen, they allowed Mrs Appenzeller to be the first to step ashore. What is factual, however, is that there has long been a great spirit of co-operation between the different missionaries, and women have always been very much in the forefront of things concerning Korean church growth.

Another proven fact is that the Methodists introduced the concept of the Wesleyan Class Meeting to Korea, and by the turn of the century they were using it successfully to nurture small groups under local lay leadership. Yonggi Cho has certainly perfected the house-cell system to a new level of effectiveness, but he has never claimed to be the originator of it. It is widely acknowledged that the Wesleyan Class Meeting has made a major contribution to the growth of the Korean church. The system has been adopted by nearly every donomination in Korea; most have adapted it slightly to suit their own particular needs, but the basic principles are the same.

In the post-Korean War era, the Chung Hyeon Presbyterian Church is a shining example of using cell groups. This church was founded in 1953 by the Revd Kim Chang-in with eighteen people, of whom most, like himself, were dedicated believers who had fled from North Korea in quest of freedom for their faith. Today there is a membership in excess of 10,000. The Revd Kim Chang-in is yet another brilliant luminary among the galaxy of great Korean ministers. By the time he was twenty-three he was already leading other Christians in the fight on the Shinto shrine issue in the days of Japanese occupation. When the communists took over North Korea in 1945 he bravely resisted their intrigues also, until his flight for freedom brought him to Seoul. He has pastored his church for over thirty years, and was honoured by being elected as moderator of the Presbyterian Church in 1970. Although suffering with tuberculosis since childhood, he has never allowed this to hinder him from strenuously serving God.

By 1955 Kim Chang-in had sixteen cell groups. (Yonggi Cho did not begin his house-cell system until 1964.) Ever since 1973 Chung Hyeon Church has trained cell-group leaders on the basis of a regular curriculum. This covers a wide variety of topics: how to study the Bible; worship and godly living; Christian fellowship; Presbyterian doctrine; stewardship; personal evangelism; follow-up of new Christians; home visitation; the cell-group system; and Christian social life. The effectiveness of the training is revealed by the increase in cells, which had reached 631 in 1983.

His cell groups are based on a unit of five families. His cell-group leaders are soul-winners and ever on the alert for opportunities to witness presented by such occasions as funerals, weddings and sixtieth-birthday celebrations. (The sixtieth birthday is one of three days which Koreans celebrate in a very special way, the others being one hundred days and one year.)

In the last ten years Chung Hyeon Church has been engaged in a most ambitious construction programme involving an education building and a mission centre building, as well as a new main sanctuary. The cost, some fifteen million US dollars, has been met entirely from within the membership. They now have one of the biggest church complexes not only in Korea but in all Asia.

As may be expected, the famous Kwang Lim Methodist Church under the dynamic leadership of the Revd Dr Kim Sun-Do makes much of the cell-group system. They now have around 1,000 cell groups which meet on a weekly basis. They aim for a group size of five to seven families. When a group reaches ten families it divides. Dr Kim Sun-Do declares that his church has experienced renewal in prayer, Bible study and fellowship through this revival of the Wesleyan Class Meeting. As he is a medical man as well as a theologian, it is instructive to find that he encourages prayer for the sick in these small groups. He states that a number of people in his church have been healed through the intercession of those within their own group. This promotes not only healing but also a healthy spiritual attitude within the group and the church, making for faith rather than superstition, and focusing attention on the Lord himself as the healer rather than on the minister or evangelist.

Not surprisingly, when it comes to cell groups the equally famous Young Nak Presbyterian Church in Seoul is another strong and practical advocate. Like Chung Hyeon Church, Young Nak Church was established by devout refugees from North Korea. In this case it was started in 1945 by the Revd Han Kyung-Chik with a couple of dozen fellow refugees who had fled South from the Russians. It quickly became a Mecca for the growing number of refugees from North Korea, and as early as 1947 they were having to hold multiple services to accommodate the crowds. They had just completed their fine new sanctuary in June 1950 when the North Koreans invaded, forcing Han Kyung-Chik and his congregation to flee for their lives yet again. However, just as the first persecution of the early church by Saul of Tarsus succeeded only in scattering the fire, so it was in this case. The congregation was dispersed through several cities mainly in the extreme south of the country, and they succeeded in planting 'Young Nak' churches in many of them. These continued with a nucleus of local converts after the war ended in 1953 and the refugees had returned to Seoul.

During their absence the communists took possession of the new Young Nak sanctuary and used it as an ammunition dump. When finally forced to retreat northwards, the communists started a fire with a view to blowing up the sanctuary and destroying the remaining ammunition at the same time. However, by an overruling miracle the fire went out leaving the building intact. Han Kyung-Chik and his restored congregation soon set to and cleaned the sanctuary in preparation for its dedication in 1954.

In building up the congregation to its present strength of over 60,000 members, cell groups have played a vital part. Dr Han was made pastor emeritus in 1973 and Dr Park Cho-Choon, who took over as senior pastor, has continued to develop the cell groups. The large congregation comes from a wide area and the city has been divided into about a score of subdistricts, each with approximately 1,000 families and a full-time, ordained minister. Their cells are slightly bigger ones of around twelve families. The 1,500 cell leaders meet every Monday morning at the church to receive the Bible teaching for their cells.

Although Yonggi Cho did not start house cells until 1964, he now has over 43,000 cells and in excess of 50,000 house-cell leaders. Yonggi Cho did not even consider house cells until the pressure of trying to cope with a rapidly growing church by the traditional one-man ministry method brought him to the point of collapse in 1964. By then he had a congregation of about 3,000 members, but his ambition was to have a church bigger than Young Nak Presbyterian Church, which was then the city's largest with 6,000 members. Pray, preach, strive as he might he could not get beyond 3,000 members; the work had reached a plateau. One Sunday after six years of almost ceaseless, frenzied activity his weak body could stand no more. That morning he had preached in three consecutive services; in the afternoon he personally baptised by immersion around 200 new converts; in the evening, as he was interpreting for a visiting American evangelist, he collapsed on the platform and had to be rushed to hospital.

Forced to rest at last, God began to speak to him. Cell groups had not been on the curriculum at the Bible Institute, but the principle was first tried by Moses after he was brought to the brink of a breakdown in a similar 'one man does it all' situation. On the advice of his father-in-law, Moses started to delegate, setting leaders over thousands, hundreds and tens. Yonggi Cho realised that he had to take the risk of trusting other people to share in leadership. During this period of enforced rest he came to realise that although he was baptised with the Holy Spirit and spoke in tongues, he needed to recognise in a much more definite way that the Holy Spirit is a Person, a real Person, a very special Person. He began to cultivate close communion with the Spirit of God. It was a turning point in his ministry.

He thought through very carefully the concept of cell

groups meeting in homes and then shared it with his deacons and deaconesses. The deacons, especially, raised all kinds of obstacles and in the end it was the deaconesses who led the way to success with cells—the men meekly followed after being shown the way by the women.

Prior to this Yonggi Cho thought that the way to successful evangelism was to bring in outstanding evangelists, advertise widely, organise an attractive programme and results were assured. From his own experience and after much heartache he at last learned otherwise. Around the time that he moved from his tent church to Sodaemoon to pioneer his second church, he became linked with a special outreach organised by the American Assemblies of God. They felt that Yonggi Cho was the right person for the project they had in mind. As part of their ambitious world missionary vision called 'Global Conquest' they were raising money to erect a 2,000–seater revival centre in Seoul. An American missionary duly arrived to pilot the scheme and in time the auditorium was ready. Now all they had to do was fill it. When a big-name speaker came, people flocked in, but when the famous preacher departed so did the people, and Yonggi Cho often found himself preaching to a near-empty auditorium, his only congregation a few old ladies huddled together under the pulpit, most contriving to doze off when he started to preach. He was learning all about the major problem of modern evangelism: follow-up.

It must be said that even before he started the house cells, Yonggi Cho experienced good results from his own ministry as he began to 'visualise' and 'dream of seeing the place full'. By 1964 he had succeeded in filling the auditorium, but doing it on the basis of one-man ministry meant a breakdown was inevitable. Since then he has not had any more evangelistic crusades or put on special programmes to attract people; he has built up the work to its present amazing strength through the regular ministry of his own church, especially the house cells.

It is not within the scope of this book to trace the evolution of the house-cell system at Yoido Full Gospel Church from its small beginnings to its present huge size. We shall, therefore, have to content ourselves with highlighting the main elements of the house-cell operation as we found it. To say that the organisation is staggering is a gross understatement. The smooth efficiency with which this mammoth operation is undertaken would be a credit to any of the world's most famous and efficient business houses. In June 1987 when we were there, the whole of the city was divided into twenty-one subdistricts, but continued growth means that another new district is on the point of being created, making twenty-two. The whole operation is computerised using the latest large computer units to ensure speed and efficiency. Yonggi Cho himself heads the whole thing because he believes that this is so important it must have maximum backing from the main pastor. At least twice a year he runs a three-day conference for cell leaders and lectures personally at some point during the programme, seeking to motivate the leaders and to impress upon them how important every one of them is to him.

Immediately under him is the director of pastoral care, and then next come the twenty-one district leaders, all ordained ministers. Some of these men have as many as 30,000 people under their care, which means they have to be outstanding in every way to be entrusted with such responsibility. Over the years this great church has had its problems, difficulties and even disagreements among the elders and deacons, but they have never had a split. That in itself is an outstanding miracle which Yonggi Cho attributes to prayer.

Each of the districts has its own separate office located in the basement of the main sanctuary. To enter any one of these is like entering a military strategy room. They all have maps and charts on the wall, and the general air of efficiency which pervades everything indicates total dedication to the task of winning souls for Jesus. Offices are fully manned throughout normal office hours of 9 am to 5.30 pm, and good staff discipline is maintained. One, by no means junior, staff member was allotted to us one afternoon to help us with our assignment of gathering material for this book. He was most helpful, but when we wanted him to take us to a Christian centre which was off the premises he quickly informed us that he was not allowed to leave the area during office hours. Records of the more than half a million members are kept up to date, and they claim to be able to trace any individual very quickly. All the districts are further divided into anything from eleven to eighteen subdistricts. Each subdistrict has its own leader who comes under the authority of the district leader. The subdistricts are further divided into about fourteen sections, each with its own section leader. Each section contains from five to fifteen house cells, and each house cell is composed of members from five to ten households. In January 1987 there were 336 subdistrict leaders; 5,042 section leaders, 46,208 house cell leaders and 46,208 assistant house cell leaders.

We soon discovered that another of the elements in all this is the marvellous leadership training plan. Every cell leader has been trained; furthermore, no one is allowed to lead one without first having served as an assistant leader. When he first started his house cells, Yonggi Cho did not know anything about training workers—he just appointed people he thought were suitable and left them to it. He soon discovered the need for training when he got the feedback from some of the teaching being given. One cell leader, in trying to teach her group about the Trinity, described God as having one body and three heads, and was in danger of giving the impression that God was a monster. He therefore instituted a suitable training programme, which as well as including a good initial period with a set curriculum, also provides an excellent on-going programme of continual education.

There is a six-month programme in the Lay Christians Bible School and this programme is available during both the day and the evening, ensuring that all have a chance to attend. After they have successfully completed the six-month course, cell leaders move on to a one-year course in the Lay Bible College. Then they continue their studies for another year in the Lay Bible Graduate Course. By the time they have completed this training the cell leaders are effective workers. But that is not the end of it: every Sunday after the services there is a seminar for cell leaders. And after all that, there is still more. The church's own Bible Institute produces all their teaching material, and every six months they produce a new textbook for the cell leaders. This ensures that all the teaching is biblical, faith building, and in accordance with the preaching given from the main pulpit by Yonggi Cho and the select group of twenty-two ordained ministers who share the platform ministry with him. Yonggi Cho spends a great deal of time with these particular ministers, most of whom are quite young. He somehow finds the time to meet them regularly on a one-to-one basis as well as in the group. This is another secret behind the success of this great church.

Yonggi Cho made the startling confession that he is a very poor personal soul-winner! (It is this quality of humble frankness, this willingness to bare his soul and share the inmost secrets of his heart which I found so endearing, and which I believe reveals the true greatness of the man.) He says:

'I am very timid. I can preach very boldly in the pulpit, but God has not given me the gift of evangelism. My inner soul cringes with fear when I try to personally witness to someone.'

The successful personal soul-winners in his church are the house-cell leaders. He is always on the lookout for men or women cell leaders who show they have a special gift for personal evangelism.

One day he received a phone call from a cell leader asking him if he would please come and speak to her house cells. He laughed kindly as he explained that as she well knew, he never went to speak at the house cells because if he went to one and the news leaked out, all the others would expect him to go, and with nearly 50,000 house cells that was impossible. Out of interest he asked her how many she had in her house cells. He was staggered when she told him that she had 5,000 in the cells which she had started in her area, which was Inchon, some miles away from Seoul. He asked her which church they attended on Sundays and could hardly believe it when she told him they all attended Yoido every week on buses which she organised. In view of that, he promised he would not only go out and preach for her but he would help to organise a church out there and would provide an ordained minister. It was not very long before they had their own building with a congregation which had doubled to 10,000.

About three years ago another of his women cell leaders won 364 families to the Lord in one year. That is very exceptional of course, even for Yoido Full Gospel Church; on average a cell leader wins ten people to the Lord each year. Every house cell is set a definite goal of winning two families every year. Yonggi Cho further pinpoints a definite target for them by asking the cell leader to appoint a candidate family in their neighbourhood whom they want to win for Christ. They then pray specifically for this family in the cell meeting and will seek for opportunities to share the love of Christ with them.

Our being in Seoul at the start of the student demonstrations in June 1987 hindered us in some ways but helped in others, in that it afforded us the opportunity to see how the Christians reacted under pressure. By sharing our experiences with the four postgraduate students from America who were on a special assignment from Oral Roberts University to study the Yoido church, and especially the house cells, we were able to gain a valuable insight into cell life at the grass roots. One thing which emerged very clearly was that the district leaders and subdistrict leaders are true pastors with caring hearts for the flocks. All kinds of people attend Yoido Full Gospel Church, from the poorest of the poor to millionaires, from the uneducated to university professors. All receive the personal and special care they need. (We sometimes forget that the very rich and the highly educated also have their own peculiar problems.) One evening when a subdistrict had organised an all-night prayer session at Prayer Mountain, the leader arrived with the bus to pick up people from one area only to find they were right in the middle of a student demonstration which was beginning to look rather ugly. Police in riot gear were lined up and tear gas was already filling the air with its pungent sting. His people wanted to come out but were afraid. The leader walked through the middle of the danger area and led those of his people who wanted to pray out of their streets and on to the buses.

On another occasion, at the end of a day's visiting in one poor area the subdistrict leader and one of the students came across three or four families who had just been evicted from their homes by their landlords and were there in the middle of the street with their furniture. The mother in one group was not only from Yoido Full Gospel Church but had recently become a cell leader. The subdistrict leader immediately took positive steps to give financial assistance and back-up with food, as well as praying and providing support in every way possible. They returned next day and all were thrilled when the mother reported how God had answered prayer for them; a former employer of her husband had got to hear of their plight and had offered the man a job with accommodation for the family. Such things bind people together in love and provide a positive demonstration of Christianity in action to a society which is still predominantly heathen but which is being won over by the greatest miracle of all: the love of Jesus in his people.

In 1986 when a great flood caused havoc in some parts of the city, Yoido Full Gospel Church was able to say that none of its members who had been forced to leave their homes had needed to go into schools or public buildings. They were all cared for by members of their house cells, who housed them, fed them and cared for them, and when the flood waters subsided had also helped to clean up the houses and redecorate them to make them fit for habitation again. No wonder such a church just keeps on growing and growing. Yonggi Cho describes his church as the smallest as well as the biggest church in the world— because every member is part of a house cell. And every one of his members is inspired to be a missionary to his neighbours and God's agent for revival in that locality.

13

The Miracle of 'All Means' Evangelism

By 'all means' I mean all. The scope of the Korean church's evangelism staggered me. In their zeal to win souls to Christ I discovered that they use surely every means, ancient and modern, ever exploited by evangelists. I could not think of any method they had not mastered and perfected to the nth degree.

There is much more to church growth in Korea than prayer and cell groups. They preach and practise every method of soul-winning from personal evangelism to mass evangelism—and by 'mass' I mean crowds in excess of a million on numerous occasions. They use radio and television (no expense spared) with an expertise and a professionalism which surpasses anything I know of in Europe. They produce their own literature for evangelism which is of the highest quality. They use telephone ministry more extensively than anything I have found in Britain. And I could go on. It all left me feeling very much as the Queen of Sheba must have felt after visiting Solomon to find out whether the reports she had heard were true; having seen it for herself 'there was no more spirit in her'. She was forced to confess: 'behold, the half was not told me: thy wisdom and prosperity exceedeth the fame which I heard' (1 Kings 10:5, 7).

Witnessing is a high priority for Korean Christians of all denominations. 'Start as you mean to go on' is an excellent maxim and one that the first missionaries seem to have followed concerning soul-winning. As soon as a Korean came to trust Jesus through the gospel of salvation, he was encouraged to begin witnessing. This kind of evangelism was established from the first and has become traditional in the Korean church. Korean churches have drummed it into every new believer that they must witness for Jesus from the moment of their salvation. Personal evangelism has been made a very important subject in churches and in Christian schools. As mentioned earlier, in the early days of the work, to be catechised by a church a person had to lead at least one other to Christ before membership was granted.

A person being catechised is a catechumen, that is one who promises to lead a Christian life, regularly attending worship services and studying prescribed biblical material in order to be examined for church membership six months after being admitted to the catechumenate. Although this is essentially a Presbyterian concept, it has been adopted with variations by most churches; commitment is demanded before one is considered for membership.

Even in these days of the mass media, personal evangelism remains the most fruitful form of all in Korea. This was demonstrated most effectively way back in 1910, just three years after the great revival. Burdened for the nation, the Protestant churches and missions in Korea organised a united effort to win a 'Million Souls for Christ' in a period of twelve months. However, in spite of being superbly organised, well supported and much prayed over, the end results were disappointing. Millions of tracts were distributed, and 700,000 copies of Mark's Gospel were bought by Koreans. The best preachers poured out their hearts. In the providence of God, the famous and successful evangelistic duo of Wilbur Chapman and Charles Alexander arrived in Seoul on the very day the campaign was agreed upon and given a name. They inspired the missionaries and fired them for the great task ahead, and left behind an experienced member of their team, George T B Davis, to assist on a long-term basis. There was no shortage of enthusiasm from those who participated, and many decisions were made, but the target fell well short of the ambitious one million. Actual figures are difficult to come by, but though much good was undoubtedly done and the 'seed of the word' was faithfully sown on a wide scale across the nation, the lasting visible results were acknowledged to be disappointing. Discerning missionaries felt that it was proof that the Korean Christians' indigenous method of 'constant, individual personal work' was far superior to the Western one of highly organised public evangelistic meetings.

It is also interesting, and something to reflect upon, that the few churches which were pastored by Westerners in the pre-Korean War era were the slowest in their growth. In the post-Korean War period it has also been noted that wherever and whenever there has been too much Western interference and influence it has only succeeded in slowing down church growth.

Throughout their long history the Korean people have been very family centred, and this has assisted personal evangelism. When once a member of a family has found Christ, they immediately want to win their whole family for Christ. Not that this is always easy. If the father is the first to be converted, then because of his accepted position as head, the rest of the family may well follow his example and all turn to Christ. But if one of the children is the first to come to Christ it can be very difficult initially, as in the case of Yonggi Cho, who was turned out of his home and on to the streets by his Buddhist family. However, his faithfulness was rewarded and today it is worth recording that no less than seventy members of the Cho 'clan' have become Christians, and of the direct family twenty have been saved, seven now being pastors. Let no one think that it is easy in Korea to win one's family. It can be very costly indeed; it certainly means that new converts have to live the Christian life at home and pray much if they are to succeed in winning their family for Christ. The fact that so many succeed is proof of the reality of their conversion and the power and effectiveness of personal soul-winning.

The testimony of a young minister in full-time service at Yoido Full Gospel Church, Pastor Young Joon Kim, illustrates the point that it is no easier to win souls in Korea than in Britain or America. Pastor Young Joon Kim told me that his family was Buddhist. When he was in his senior year at university he was like most of the other students, smoking and drinking, and then one day his girlfriend invited him to accompany her to a meeting at which Dr Yonggi Cho was preaching. She had come to know about Jesus through her sister. At the first meeting Joon Kim thought, 'I am just a small sinner,' and he felt quite free to criticise others. Dr Cho preached on the incident of the woman taken in adultery in John 8, and stressed the words of Jesus 'He that is without sin among you, let him first cast a stone at her.'

In the time of prayer following the appeal, Joon Kim said that as he prayed he had a vision in which he saw a bright light from the multitude all around him who were praying, but his own light was dim, and this caused him to weep. He made some form of commitment to Christ but for a year he wandered and was very much half-and-half. Then he went to Prayer Mountain and spent a week praying and fasting, and that was the turning-point in his life. Soon afterwards he was invited to a party by his university friends and he witnessed boldly, but when he was offered a drink of vodka he accepted and before the end of the party he was drunk. He was ashamed of himself and disappointed at this sad failure. He had tried so hard—but it was mostly his own efforts and in his own strength.

Disillusioned, he was in a turmoil for six weeks, but then God met him and he was baptised in the Holy Spirit. He stopped smoking and drinking and from then on lived a consistent Christian life. Ultimately he felt the call of God on his life and began to prepare himself for service. He set out to win his Buddhist parents but this took time. Following Yonggi Cho's example he 'visualised' his father's conversion, picturing him in his mind's eye with a Bible. For over a year he prayed in this way, while his father continued to 'intone his own prayers' as a devout Buddhist.

The 'womb' Christian concept is practised by Korea's Total Evangelisation Movement and is not peculiar to Yonggi Cho's church. The idea is that every Christian should pray for and become involved with a non-Christian until they are brought to a new-birth experience. I do not think that the Apostle Paul would have had any difficulty with this concept, in view of his words to the Galatians about travailing in birth again until Christ was formed in them (Gal 4:19).

Joon Kim's mother was the first to accept Christ, which she did shortly before her death. It was her death which God used to break down his father's resistance, and he too yielded his life to Christ. Joon Kim said that he was with his father when he was dying, and in the corner of his father's room he saw a light which he took as a symbol of God's mercy and a reassurance that his father was truly born again. This kind of mysticism is strange to the majority of Westerners, but it has always been a feature of Welsh Christianity, especially in times of revival. The spiritual world (both good and bad) is very real to most Koreans, whereas Western Christianity has become so materialistic and intellectual that all such phenomena are treated with suspicion, if not outright dismissal.

In 1979 Young Joon Kim started working full time in the telephone counselling service at Yoido Full Gospel Church, and was eventually made managing director.

This vital ministry is just another example of Korean thoroughness in exploiting to the full every means to win souls. One aspect of the phone ministry is the use of automatic answering machines, where callers can listen to a short recorded message from Yonggi Cho. In the sixteen-month period between February 1986 and May 1987 they received over half a million calls. (The actual number of calls was 537,422. Meticulous record-keeping is an outstanding feature of the big churches in Korea.) Another line offers callers a short programme of praise and music.

On 5th May 1980 they inaugurated the Agape Line, which is manned around the clock and offers callers a personal counselling service. This is run by volunteers who work in three-hour shifts, plus three or four full-time staff. All are trained to deal with problems ranging from family matters to those relating to the Christian life. The Agape Line is obviously meeting a real need because they deal with over seventy calls per day, 90 per cent of them from Christians with problems. In the first six years of operating this service they dealt with over 120,000 calls. Some of these calls may take up to an hour or more.

Pastor Young Joon Kim had been working in the Evening Bible School for two years at the time of our interview, but he informed us that very shortly he would be going to Hong Kong as a missionary and was already studying the language in preparation. When we asked him about how he received his call to Hong Kong he informed us that his 'call' came through an order from Dr Yonggi Cho, who simply told him that he wanted him to go to Hong Kong as a missionary in three months' time. Without any demurring he accepted this directive. He has a young wife and a new baby, and though it is not going to be easy they are all going believing that God will help them to start a new work there. The terms on which he goes are the same for all who are sent out from Yoido: they will be supported for six months only, by which time they are expected to have gathered a group around them, through establishing house cells, who will support them. Personal soul-winning has to work or else . . . And it does, even in the hardest places.

Yonggi Cho told us of sending one of his Korean women pastors to pioneer a work in the difficult area of Ginza in Tokyo. I know from several of my missionary friends who spent years in Japan just how hard that field is. But this woman, by renting a small house and inviting her neighbours to worship in her home, started a house cell. After a year she had 180 members, and now is the official pastor of a new church. Another woman pastor from Cho's church succeeded in doing something similar in Taipei, Taiwan, which I know from more of my missionary friends is also a very difficult place. Yet within three months this woman pastor had gathered fifty Chinese as members of her house cell.

The best personal soul-winners in Korea have been women—and this in spite of the fact that women in the Orient are held in low regard. When visiting England in 1981, Yonggi Cho personally expressed to me his surprise and sorrow on finding that in the liberated West, where women are treated much more as equals, the churches did not use women nearly as much as in Korea. Howbeit, when these Korean women come to the Western world they do not let that inhibit them. All the cell leaders at Yoido are given a special cell leaders' handbag. This is easily recognised by the symbol embossed on it, and it has become very much a 'badge of office'. In New York airport on one occasion, Yonggi Cho happened to meet a woman carrying one of these bags. He discovered that although she had emigrated to New York she still regarded herself as one of his cell leaders. On coming to New York she had opened her home and set out to 'catch' her neighbours for Jesus, and she was succeeding in bringing them to believe in Jesus as lord and saviour. There are more than seventy Korean churches in America

which have links with Yoido Full Gospel Church, and all
but two or three have been started by cell leaders who,
on emigrating, have opened up their new homes and set
out to win their neighbours for Christ. The key is personal
soul-winning.

Successful soul-winners use wisdom. In Korea,
although society is changing rapidly it is still quite structured, and soul-winning Christians recognise this and
work accordingly. The traditional order of social rank in
Korea puts the scholar at the top of the pile and then the
student, followed by the farmer, the artisan, the merchant,
the military man, the kisaeng (the Korean equivalent of
the Japanese geisha girls), musicians and dancers, and
finally the butchers; and even among butchers there is
rank. The beef butcher is highest, next comes the pork
butcher, and the lowest of all is the dog butcher. The
butchers have been the outcasts of Korean society for over
500 years because of the Buddhist teaching against killing
animals. They were regarded as being so low as to be
classed as 'unpersons'—and unpersons in Korea do not
even belong to the human race but come somewhere
between man and monkey.

It is quite a shock to find that in certain senses foreigners are classed as 'unpersons', along with beggars, prosti-
tutes, criminals and butchers! Britishers since the days of
the Empire have tended to feel somewhat superior to the
'ignorant heathen' in distant lands. It is a surprise to find
oneself in a position where the roles are reversed; and not,
it must be said, without some justification. It is humbling
to discover that there was an early stone astronomical
observatory at Kyungju dating back to 647 AD. Rain
gauges were widely used in several provinces in 1442, 200
years ahead of Europe. Movable type for printing was
being used as early as 1250—a long, long time before
Gutenberg. Not to mention their ancient paintings, and
their rare craftsmanship which produced some of the finest
porcelain in the world. Even the famous and lovely

Satsuma porcelain of Japan was and is produced by descendants of Korean potters who were transported to Japan at the end of the sixteenth century. The Koreans are a proud, noble and intelligent race.

The early missionaries soon discovered the strength of the class differences for themselves. When a second church was opened in Seoul in 1893 (the Kongdangkol Church), in the first year it had a membership of forty-three. But in the second year, when a butcher called Pak was converted and joined the church, several of the 'upper class' left. They said they had willingly endured the presence of servants and other lower-class people in the church, but a butcher was too much for them to accept. The missionary connected with the church, the Revd S F Moore, was very interested in the butchers and was intent on raising their status in life. He succeeded in so far as thirty butchers were baptised in the first four years of the church, but the presence of so many butchers limited the growth because of the stigma.

The widespread effect of the gospel has drastically changed things, but even so, the wisdom of Christians trying to win their own peer group to the Lord has been encouraged and has proved successful. The fast-growing Chung Hyeon Presbyterian Church in Seoul has already been mentioned. In 1966 they set up a committee whose aim was to evangelise the policemen throughout the nation. They then saw the golden opportunity which the army presents. They began to train the soldiers who attended their church to win others. This was so fruitful that on 25th April 1972 the pastors of the church had the thrilling privilege of baptising 3,473 soldiers on that one day. Others have caught the vision and seen the possibilities in national service, which is compulsory for all young men: they must serve one year in the army, navy or air force. In 1984 it was claimed that 45 per cent of the soldiers were born-again believers. The Chung Hyeon Church is surrounded by markets, and many of the members did business there. These Christian merchants were soon preaching the gospel to their fellow traders and leading many of them to Christ. It was the same with the office workers—they were encouraged to win their fellow workers to the Lord.

The peer-group principle is also widely practised in the setting up of cell groups by the various churches. Yoido Full Gospel Church has many such specialised groups. In one area where there happens to be quite a concentration of women secretaries, they discovered that their best time for a cell meeting was during the lunch hour. But the secret is that these are never allowed to become 'holy huddles' because they are always on the alert to win their unsaved friends from the offices. Factory workers do something similar. In one of the largest chocolate factories in Seoul, many workers are members of Yoido Full Gospel Church. They approached the management for permission to hold cell meetings. These are flourishing, and the members impressed the management so much (by increased production) that the manager wanted to speak to Yonggi Cho.

It is amazing to discover how many universities and colleges there are in Seoul, and in other parts of the country also. Several groups are promoting personal evangelism among the students. Yoido have their own Campus Crusade mission which is entitled 'Christ Ambassadors' Mission'. This department works among some fifty universities and colleges, mainly in Seoul, Inchon and Suwon.

Yoido Church also have a Youth Mission Fellowship for young working people, providing them with fellowship, training and opportunities for evangelism. Youth Mission Fellowship holds a nationwide interdenominational fasting prayer rally every year. They also use the cell-group principle for the 5,800 young people who are members, and these meet in 763 cells centring around Seoul. They hold regular evangelistic meetings.

There is also special ministry to the deaf, and this has 600 members. A regular silent language worship service is held for them, and all ages are catered for from Sunday School through middle- and high-school departments, youth and finally adults.

The peer-group principle is worked through with the Koinonia (fellowship) Mission for college and university graduates under thirty-five years of age. The concept behind Koinonia Mission is to provide training for this gifted group to produce lay leaders of the church and develop their faith. It holds weekly lectures on Christian themes and supports the sending of lay missionaries. Its foreign language service department (which at present concentrates on Japanese, English and Chinese), is very active in world missions. There are over 120 university and college professors and lecturers in Yoido Full Gospel Church and their special club, Logos Mission, meets weekly for Bible study. They also play an important role in evangelism on the campuses.

Other groups include Korea Culture and Art Mission, which was established in 1982 for those engaged in the literary and art fields. It holds an annual exhibition of poetry and printing to promote Christian culture, and propagates the gospel through the mass media, especially newspapers and radio. Teachers' Mission is interdenominational and is composed of teachers of the three levels of primary, middle and high schools; they hold an annual prayer and fasting meeting. Businessmen and their wives are specially catered for in the Korean Chapter of Yoido's own Church Growth International. The Korean Chapter support all the activities of the parent group, but in addition they award scholarships to students at Yoido Church. The Legal Profession Mission was established to promote the spread of the gospel among lawyers; they also give counsel to lay Christians in matters relating to law and tax, and they hold seminars on law and legal issues.

The Success Club World Mission (interdenominational) consists of leading Christians from all walks of
life who co-operate on matters of mutual interest, business
and jobs on the basis of mature faith. They give scholarships to local and overseas students, support the television
ministry, and provide literature for pioneer churches in
remote areas of Korea or overseas. The Glory Mission
comprises some 500 men and women over sixty years of
age. (Life expectancy is considerably below that of the
West and those who make it to sixty command special
respect.) Their slogan is 'Let's be renewed by faith.' As
well as visiting eventide homes they have established a
college for the aged especially to teach the Bible, hymns
and cultural subjects.

Having mentioned mass evangelism somewhat nega-
tively in the early part of this chapter, it would be unfair
to close without recording some of the positive gains in
this area. The goal of the Korean church since liberation
from the Japanese in 1945 has been the complete evangelisation of the nation. In that year the pastor of the
Namdaemoon Presbyterian Church, the Revd Kim Chi
Sun, proposed a Three Million Evangelisation Movement.
The population was then thirty million, of which only
about 300,000 were Christians. Twenty years later, in
1965, the Revd Han Kyung-Chik and Dr Helen Kim
developed a Thirty Million to Christ Korean evangelisation movement.

In 1973 Korea grabbed the attention of Christians
worldwide when they staged their largest mass rally—of
one million—during the Billy Graham Crusade on the
now famous Yoido Plaza. This vast open space on Yoido
island in the River Han was used as an airstrip by the
United Nations Air Force during the Korean War. After
the war and the erection of the National Assembly
building on Yoido island, the great concrete runway
which had been used by the famous American 'Flying
Fortress' bombers, was turned into a plaza for the public

of Seoul. Just across one of the main roads which runs parallel with the Plaza is the Korean War Museum, where all the various types of aeroplanes, bombers and fighters, used in that war are preserved as museum pieces, along with an imposing array of tanks (from both armies) and other items, including a moving display of photographs depicting the horrors of that gruesome conflict.

In the election campaign for the presidency in December 1987, all the three main candidates staged political rallies in the Plaza where they gathered crowds of one million—although news correspondents reported that many were bribed to attend, or even worse, threatened if they did not. However, no such compulsion has been necessary for the Christians to fill the Plaza on several other auspicious occasions since Billy Graham's 1973 crusade.

The year following the crusade, many churches united to stage EXPLO '74. Under the inspiring leadership of Dr Kim Joon-Gon, the national director of Korea Campus Crusade for Christ, they set about the mammoth task of training 300,000 Christians to win souls. (There were then an estimated three million Christians in Korea.) On the first night of this crusade on the Plaza there was an audience of 1.3 million. The response to the invitation to receive Christ exceeded expectations. Thousands more made professions of faith as the 323,400 trainees from seventy-eight countries carried out personal evangelism on the streets of Seoul throughout the week. A year later, a survey of 1,000 churches revealed a 33 per cent increase in church attendance between July 1974 and July 1975. By the end of the decade it was estimated that the Christian population had increased to seven million. During this same period, by training leaders and letting them plant new churches in their own villages, the Hap-Tong Presbyterian denomination established 1,200 churches in two years, so that by January 1976 they had 2,484 churches. By November 1978 they had grown to 3,884 churches, and their membership had almost doubled in this overall period from 680,000 to one million.

In 1980, over 90 per cent of the churches across the nation united for World Evangelisation Crusade. Total attendances at the Yoido Plaza rallies were 10.5 million (over 2 million nightly), and 5.2 million were at all-nights of prayer (At one of the largest of these, over 1.5 million Christians prayed all night in the Plaza.) One million made professions of salvation, and a further one million Christians made a missionary pledge.

At the historic Centennial Year of Protestant Missions in 1984, the Plaza was again filled night after night with over a million people during the week of celebrations, and with over a million people also staying to pray all night in the rain. The climax was a vast evangelistic rally addressed by Billy Graham.

Before the end of this century the Korean church is determined to achieve national evangelisation with more than fifty per cent of the nation Christian, as well as believing and praying for a miracle in North Korea which will see that part of the nation liberated. Christian leaders, such as the Baptist Billy Kim (who was educated in America), are actively engaged in Christian broadcasting to the communist North and to other communist countries. The ultimate goal is world evangelisation, and more and more Korean Christians are volunteering to work overseas on a short-term or long-term basis. Their commitment to evangelism, far from diminishing, is increasing all the time.

14

The Miracle of God's Unfailing Grace

The spirit of Korean Christians today can be summed up as follows. They believe that: 'Christians should go forth as seeing the invisible, believing the incredible, and doing the impossible.' Their attitude is: 'You don't test the resources of God until you attempt the impossible so that, unless God is in it, it is doomed to failure.' In almost every way the situation in Korea today is impossible, but the Korean church has learned to live with the impossible and to draw by faith upon the infinite resources of the Lord God Almighty.

Take the election for president on 16th December 1987 and the troubles and demonstrations before and after: the student demonstrations, the riot police and the tear gas, the accusations of ballot rigging and cheating; all these things combined to create a crisis which the world's media reported with alarm. Make no mistake, it was serious, and the Christians were not complacent; but they were amazingly calm. Their attitude was: 'We have seen it all before and God has undertaken and will undertake as we are faithful.' The real battle was never reported in the world's media. Behind the scenes millions of Christians in Korea refused to be drawn into the demonstrations but instead gave themselves to nights of prayer and days of fasting and seeking the face of God. Of course some sections of the church got involved in the demonstrations, but the believing, born-again, Spirit-filled nucleus of the Korean church refused to be diverted from their high calling, knowing that the real issue was one of spiritual warfare.

This does not mean that the church in Korea is so heavenly minded that it is no earthly use. Far from it! The practical and social aspects of the gospel are not neglected, and the involvement of many of the churches puts the average evangelical church in the West to shame. Although the nation of Korea has made remarkable economic progress since 1953, it is still a developing country and the church is aware of the many poor people who need help. The Young Nak Presbyterian Church and Yoido Full Gospel Church both have ongoing programmes of social relief. Rice is still very much the staple food, and members of both congregations regularly bring in bags of rice which are collected together and later distributed to those in need, firstly to those in the church and then to the poor in general. It was very moving for us to go into the basement of Yoido Church one Sunday and see the women receiving the 'tithes of rice' from members. The women emptied it into large sacks, which were then stacked up and stored in readiness for distribution to the poor. They read James as well as Paul and believe that 'faith, if it hath not works, is dead, being alone' (James 2:17). Clothing is also provided for the destitute. At least once a year, Yonggi Cho will challenge the members of his congregation to go home and find a good suit with a shirt, matching tie and shoes, or dresses and items of women's clothing; no rubbish, the best they can find. They are then to get them drycleaned and bring them to the church. The clothing is distributed to those who are in need, both in the church—those unemployed or sick—and then throughout the city and out into the rural areas, where many pastors are often in great need. The distribution is not confined to their own denomination or affiliation, or to Christians: they seek to help the poor everywhere.

What does seem to be unique to Yoido Church is their commitment since 1984 to providing the finance for open-heart surgery for children with heart disease. In the three years from 1984 to 1987 they have enabled over 400 children to have this costly operation. There is no National Health Service in Korea. It is especially interesting that Yoido Church, which has such a strong belief in divine healing, is also balanced enough in their teaching to acknowledge that there is a need and a place for medicine and surgery.

It was also our privilege to see a filmed progress report of Yoido Church's latest venture into the field of social welfare. Under the banner 'Practising Love', the construction is now well advanced of an extremely ambitious project called 'Elim Welfare Town'. Situated on the outskirts of Seoul, this welfare community will provide food and shelter for a wide range of needy youth and senior citizens. We heard Yonggi Cho personally explaining to his congregation the thinking behind the scheme, which will cost a staggering 100 million pounds sterling (170 million American dollars). The Vocational Training Centre in the town will provide specialised technical training for youth who for various reasons have not received sufficient education to get any qualifications, and are therefore classed as hard core unemployed. They are confident that Elim Welfare Town will play an important role in helping needy people in Korean society.

Most of us would be more than content with such a programme, but not Yoido Church. They have also decided to construct a Workers' Welfare Town for needy women workers who earn low incomes in urban communities. This is designed to provide homes for 3,000 workers, with auxiliary facilities such as a library, lounges, and church. Even that is not the end of their planning. Under their social works programme they have already built

thirty army chapels, and subsidise about 1,000 interdenominational churches in rural and fishing villages which
are not self-supporting.

If all this sounds like Utopia you would be wrong. The
Korean nation and the Korean church still face massive
problems. In all that was written and said about the
elections in Korea in 1987, it was hard to find one good
word about their first president, Syngman Rhee. After
being elected and serving four times he was finally
deposed in 1960, when he was caught once too often with
his hand in the ballot box. There seems no doubt about
his guilt, but neither is there any real reason to question
that he was a born-again Christian. Many Korean Christians still hold his memory in high regard; they are aware
of his shortcomings and his lapses, which were not
consistent with his claims to be a born-again, committed
Methodist, but they appreciate that in spite of his
advancing years (he was seventy-three when he first came
to office in 1948) he achieved much good and laid the
foundations for a free and progressive society.

Compared with North Korea, South Korea *is* Utopia.
South Korea has become one of the greatest economic
and industrial powers in Asia. The North, under the evil
and ageing communist dictator, Kim Il-Sung, has become
nothing better than a great prison camp. It is a miserable
totalitarian state in which the individual has no rights or
freedom and exists only for the country. Since 1955 the
destruction of all religions has been Kim Il-Sung's relentless policy: Whenever a religious person is found he or
she is killed, because 'religion as the root of non-scientific
and superstitious thought must be eliminated'. It is clear
from the limited information available about this closed
society that the cult of Kim Il-Sung has surpassed the
cults of Stalin and Mao. Although officially no Christians
exist in North Korea, there is every reason to believe that
there is a secret, underground Christian movement.

We were privileged to attend the special service at

Yoido Church on Thursday 25th June—when the great church was filled to overflowing for a special evening of music and preaching—to remember the outbreak of the Korean War on that day in 1950. The surprise invasion by North Korea will never be forgotten by South Koreans. Throughout the day as we moved around the city we saw literally thousands and thousands of young schoolchildren being taken by their teachers to visit the cemeteries around the city. The children of South Korea are constantly reminded in this most graphic way of something of the cost in human lives of the freedom they enjoy.

As I waited in Yonggi Cho's impressive vestry to interview the guest speaker for the occasion, the Revd Billy Kim, a Baptist with a flourishing church in Seoul and a warm and longstanding personal friendship with Dr Cho, I was privileged to meet a refugee from North Korea. This refugee had given his testimony in the service. He told how he had got to a point where he found life unbearable under the repressive regime there and determined to escape at any cost. It meant leaving behind his mother and other loved ones but he finally escaped by swimming a river. He was three hours in the water before he made it to freedom.

The concert of sacred music that evening was something to be savoured. Leading Christian choirs, musicians and gospel singers had been assembled for this important occasion. The quality of the music in Korea (both sacred and secular) is one of the pleasant surprises that await one. The way in which Koreans have embraced and mastered Western music and made it a part of their own modern culture is yet another achievement of this versatile people. They are very musical and of course have their own traditional music and songs, but they love Western music, and their symphony orchestras, musicians and singers have taken the highest honours and can compete with any in the world. It is a wonderful fact that in Korea almost all the famous musicians are Christians. The playing of the Korean clarinettist (over from America) who gave a medley of gospel pieces that evening is something I will never forget; it was anointed in such a way that it was hauntingly beautiful. I treasure the tape he so generously presented me with and go into raptures every time I play it.

However, returning to the vexed question of free elections in Korea, and the presidency of Syngman Rhee. Christians in the West have come to realise that being born again does not in itself make one successful at any and every undertaking. A good Christian does not necessarily make a good president, or a good prime minister, or a good member of parliament; a good Christian must also gain the necessary knowledge and expertise just like any other person. Then and only then can we expect them to perform better than others with similar qualifications but who do not have the bonus of new birth.

Abraham Lincoln was a shrewd man and he wisely observed: 'Nearly all men can stand adversity, but if you want to test a man's character, give him power.' That is surely one reason why the Holy Spirit inspired the chroniclers in Old Testament times to give us the divine view of the lives and reigns of the various kings and rulers. Not even David, the man after God's own heart, comes out untarnished.

It makes little difference whether the person given power is in politics or in the church, the temptations are virtually the same. One has to be realistic and report that there are power struggles in the church in Korea. But it is thrilling to find that all the churches in Korea are full, whether it is the great churches mentioned throughout this book or the many thousands of smaller churches, scores and scores of which are in hired halls in apartment blocks, and in back streets, as well as in fine new buildings springing up on the main streets. There is a competitiveness between many of the churches which is not entirely unhealthy: it stimulates growth and they keep one another on their toes. There is also a zealousness for sound doctrine which again is good, but occasionally it gets out of hand and becomes a witch hunt and a means of people venting their personal jealousies under the cloak of orthodoxy.

It is tempting to imagine that those in the mega-churches have really made it and that all their troubles are over, but this would be a false view. To see the beautiful smile which constantly lights up the face of Yonggi Cho, you would think that he has no problems. Now that he is the pastor of the world's biggest church, you may well decide that 'he has made it' into the wonderful land of 'trouble-free'. It is only as the full story of recent days is pieced together that one appreciates the miracle of God's grace in his life that he can smile at all.

During our time in Korea we were very privileged to stay in an apartment in the Education Building which immediately adjoins the main sanctuary and affords one a grandstand view of everything that happens at this great church. It was sobering to remind ourselves that it was from the top floor of this fourteen-storey block that Yonggi Cho so nearly committed suicide in those dark days in 1970 when everything suddenly went wrong in the construction of the vast Yoido sanctuary. The world oil crisis of that time created a financial crisis, and bills were piling up. The contractor broke his agreement and the city began threatening to take action, as the rusting girders were an eyesore in the prestigious area just a few hundred yards from the National Assembly building— the Korean parliament. Defeated, dispirited, depressed, Yonggi Cho had gone to the fourteenth floor, opened a window and crawled out on the ledge. The situation was so desperate that it seemed the only way out—to jump and end it all. Then he suddenly remembered some unfinished work on his desk and he climbed back in and hurried down to his office.

Shortly afterwards God turned the situation for him,

through an old woman who responded to his challenge to give by presenting him with her only possessions—her rice bowl, chopsticks and spoon. She said that she could manage by eating out of cardboard and with her fingers. Yonggi Cho was overcome by this gesture, yet felt he could not possibly accept such a sacrifice from one so poor. But a businessman in the congregation stood up and said he wanted to buy them—and he gave a gift of hundreds of pounds for them. (He then gave them back to the old lady.) It released a new spirit of sacrificial giving and faith in the congregation; some members sold their houses and moved into rented accommodation. Nearly all the congregation made tremendous sacrifices, and this is another reason why God has so singularly blessed Yoido Church.

The period in the 1980s has been the period of greatest growth in Yonggi Cho's church; it has also been the time when he has had to endure the most cruel suffering at the hands of some of his fellow Christians. His outstanding success has always made him a target for the envious. Sadly, one of the first hurtful things to happen to him came from those with whom he was most closely linked in the Korean Fellowship of Assemblies of God. The Korean tradition of ancester worship has always been a thorny problem for the church in Korea. It seems that some of his fellow Assemblies of God pastors had been looking for anything they could seize upon to bring him down. They thought they had discovered some evidence that he had been too tolerant in the way that he had dealt with a member at Yoido over a matter relating to ancestor worship, and they were too quick to label Yonggi Cho a heretic. They succeeded in removing him from the Korean Assemblies of God. However, Yonggi Cho has been a tremendous blessing to the Assemblies of God fellowship in Australia, and they felt so strongly that he was not guilty that they afforded him special recognition with the Australian Assemblies of God.

After much hurt and heartache the matter was finally resolved and his good name was cleared. Men of international standing such as Dr Thomas Zimmerman, then the general superintendent of the American Assemblies of God, a key person in the World Pentecostal Conference and an esteemed member of the Lausanne Committee, also did much to heal the wounds and get Dr Cho reinstated. The final solution involved creating a second district in Korea, and the real truth of the matter can be seen in that many Assemblies of God churches in Korea have now switched to the district of which Yonggi Cho's church is a part; they trust him, believe in him and want to support him.

Unfortunately, the matter did not remain just a domestic affair within Assemblies of God. Other churches in Korea took the matter up and some wanted to make it a national issue and have him branded as a heretic. Some accused him of not preaching the gospel because he did not take the heavy condemnatory line so popular among many evangelicals. At the beginning of his ministry in the late 1950s, Yonggi Cho will tell you that he too preached a message that pulled down and condemned people. During that period his preaching did not win a single soul to Christ. In 1959 he developed what he calls his 'Full Gospel' message and his 'Fivefold Message of the Gospel'. He declares:

'The doctrine of "Full Gospel" is characterised by the gospel of fullness which has its foundation in the unadulterated faith of the word of God, standing on the basis of God-centred theology.'

The Fivefold Message of the Gospel is:

1. *Salvation*. The gospel of salvation is to be forgiven of sins, receive salvation and become children of God by accepting Jesus Christ as saviour, and to begin living a holy and pure life through the sealing and guidance of the Holy Spirit.

2. The Holy Spirit. Christians born again of water and of the Spirit (Jn 3:5) receive the Holy Spirit; however, they can receive the fullness of the Spirit at the time of salvation or soon after salvation. All who have received the fullness of the Holy Spirit (Acts 2:4) receive power and are witnesses of Jesus Christ (Acts 1:8). They bring forth the gifts and fruit of the Holy Spirit through the fullness of the Holy Spirit in their lives, and live a life which brings glory to God.

3. Divine Healing. One of the ministries of Jesus Christ was healing, and Christ promised, 'And these signs shall follow them that believe . . . they shall lay hands on the sick, and they shall recover' (Mk 16:17, 18). Since Jesus 'took our infirmities, and bare our sicknesses' (Mt 8:17), born-again Christians have a duty as well as a privilege to pray for the sick.

4. Blessings. Believers who receive salvation are redeemed from the curse of the law by the grace of the cross (Gal 3:13, 14). In addition, our Lord feeds and clothes believers who first seek the kingdom of God and his righteousness; and when they live for the glory of God with honesty, faithfulness, diligence and loyalty, their life will be blessed that they may live in all sufficiency. They will live a life abundant enough to share with others (2 Cor 9:8).

5. Second Coming of Jesus Christ. We believe that Christ will come to earth again: the first time his coming will be seen only by his chosen people and the second time his coming will be seen by all people on the earth. They shall attend the marriage feast of the Lamb for seven years and reign in the kingdom for 1,000 years. After the last judgement is given by him who sits upon a great white throne, they will live a glorious life forever with God in the new heaven and the new earth (Rev 21:1).

Yonggi Cho further summarises his teaching on salvation by what he calls the 'Threefold Blessings of Salvation'.

> The threefold blessings are the practical aspects of the fivefold gospel (3 Jn 2). 'Thy soul prospereth' means that by believing in Jesus Christ we live an abundant life spiritually, and 'thou mayest prosper' means that we are blessed with material things through a life in which all things work together for good. 'Thou mayest . . . be in health' means that believers who have received salvation are blessed to be delivered from the pain of sickness because Jesus paid the price of healing at Calvary.

Yoido Full Gospel Church believes its great mission is to preach the gospel of Christ to the whole world with the faith of the fivefold gospel message and the threefold blessings of salvation.

I have felt it important to give these details in full as Yonggi Cho sets them out so that readers may judge for themselves. It is not within the scope of this book to analyse them in depth. However, I do feel that it is a vital part of the Korean story that must be mentioned. Yonggi Cho believes that many ministers still keep their pulpits on Mount Sinai instead of Mount Calvary. If you ask him where sin is placed in his theology, he will tell you forthrightly that,

'Many ministers are lambasting sinners instead of lambasting sin. The danger of sin should always be proclaimed. I always preach the Ten Commandments very clearly. The holiness of God and the sin concept by the Ten Commandments should be clearly taught.'

One of the points of controversy has arisen because of what Yonggi Cho terms his respect for the self-image in every person. He preaches very clearly the blood atonement of Christ for our sins on the cross. He proclaims:

'If you remain in sin, it will finally destroy you completely and take you to hell. Get rid of the sin in your life. In Christ Jesus you can be redeemed, filled with the Holy Spirit, saved, healed, blessed, and have an eternal dwelling place in heaven.'

I was intrigued to discover in my research that Dr Paul S Crane in his little book about Korea and its traditions, *Korean Patterns* (which, first published by Paul S Crane in 1967, has become something of an established work), mentions this very thing. He states:

> Perhaps the most important thing to an individual Korean is recognition of his 'selfhood'. It is expressed in Korean by the word *kibun*, a rich word which has no true English equivalent, but relates to his awareness of being recognised as a person, his self-esteem.

Yonggi Cho has retained this approach which is so important to Koreans, and has incorporated it into his preaching without compromising the gospel.

The accusation that he was a heretic really wounded him deeply. Those near to him say that in many ways it was a crucifixion for him. He was brought low and was obviously hurting tremendously. Nevertheless, he gave himself to prayer and put his cause in the hands of God. He spent many days up at Prayer Mountain in his private grotto, fasting, humbling himself before the Lord, searching his own heart and examining his doctrines. His broadcasts on radio and television attract the largest audiences in Korea. It was both sad and amusing that while officially condemning him as a heretic, one Christian radio organisation continued to carry his programmes because of his popularity.

In the great centenary meetings in 1984, celebrating 100 years of Protestant missions in Korea, although the issue had supposedly been settled Yonggi Cho was completely ignored for a time. Then outside pressure began to mount as visitors from all over the world wanted to know when Yonggi Cho was preaching and what place he had in the celebrations. He was then brought on to the organising committee, but they still did not want him to preach. Dr Billy Graham has long been a friend and supporter of Yonggi Cho. He was the first to preach at the opening of the new church building in Yoido in 1973, and has had Yonggi Cho as a guest preacher at his great conference for evangelists in Holland. Billy Graham pressed the organisers to set their house in order before the celebrations, and so it was that Yonggi Cho did preach at one of those great gatherings on the famous Plaza. Those who were there said that there were almost as many out to hear him as for Billy Graham, and God seemed to give him an extra special anointing of the Holy Spirit, so that he was publicly vindicated in the most effective manner. Dr Billy Graham also preached at a special service in Yoido Full Gospel Church for Yonggi Cho during the celebrations which showed his support for him.

The matter flared up again in 1986 when a Korean wrote and published a book against Yonggi Cho, raking up the old issues once more and adding other things as well. It was a vilification of Yonggi Cho in a most hurtful manner, and it did indeed hurt him deeply, but once again his only response was to give himself to prayer. Furthermore, he laid the matter before his congregation and got them all praying for the author of the scandalous book. Unbeknown to them, this man visited Yoido Full Gospel Church on many occasions during this period. In such a vast crowd it is possible for people to slip in and out unnoticed. Every time this man came he heard the people and Yonggi Cho praying for him. In the end he broke down and asked if he could see Yonggi Cho, who graciously received him and expressed his forgiveness. The man asked what he could do to make amends, and agreed to destroy the remaining stocks of the book. What he could not do, of course, was recall those already sold, or undo the harm done.

I can only testify that I was personally deeply impressed by the humble and meek spirit of Yonggi Cho. Many of these details he did not give himself but were gleaned from those close to him. His answer in time of need is to give himself to prayer and let God vindicate. This has sometimes happened in ways which, while still having tragic undertones, are not without quite humorous over-tones. For example, one leading church in Seoul was very much at the centre of stirring things up against Yonggi Cho. The minister spoke so vehemently against him that some of the congregation decided they had better go along and see this terrible Yonggi Cho for themselves. Quite a crowd went to Yoido Church to hear Yonggi Cho, some of them leading members of their church. They listened in vain for the heresies of which he was accused. They enjoyed the services so much and were so blessed that many of them returned, and many of them continued coming and in the end joined Yoido Full Gospel Church.

Power struggles are not uncommon in Korea; it is part of the Korean temperament. Yonggi Cho speaks quite openly of his problems. He says:

'I am not a saint. Since I have this big church and so many elders, some days they really become a stumbling-block'. He acknowledges that he sometimes has a struggle to forgive them, but he always does because he knows it is the only way. Just a short time before our arrival in Korea, one man (not an elder, I hasten to add!) had actually told Yonggi Cho that he was going to kill him. Yonggi Cho said that when he prayed he could find it in his heart to forgive all his enemies—except this one. It took him weeks before he could really forgive the man from his heart, but he knew he had to do it if he was to keep the anointing of God on his life. Although Yonggi Cho has pioneered three churches, all of them large ones, and has had problems with his elders and deacons from time to time, he has never had a church split. He attri-butes this to one thing: prayer. This is the key to the future in Korea: as long as the praying is maintained and the spirit of forgiveness prevails, the growth will continue.

Bearing in mind the situation it was in at the end of the Korean War in 1953 and the progress made since, as a nation Korea is truly remarkable. Our visit to the magnificent Seoul Sports Complex, the stage for the twenty-fourth Olympic Games, further convinced us of the ability of this great little nation to take its place among the nations of the world. No wonder the world's athletes are delighted at the superlative stadiums, and Korea's enemies frustrated. America and the sixteen nations who fought for a free Korea under the banner of the United Nations must feel that the blood shed by the many thousands of their sons was not in vain. South Korea is now one of the greatest economic and industrial powers in Asia, and her people are hard working and learn fast.

A British businessman on the plane coming home told us of the changes he has experienced in the thirteen years he has been coming as a buyer of knitwear and fashion clothes. At first, he explained, it was a common thing to find clothes coming apart at the seams, or a sleeve coming adrift; the goods were cheap but shoddy. Today they are among the best in the world and still cheap (though wages are rising all the time and living conditions improving steadily), and many of the world's leading fashion houses have their goods manufactured in Korea. They have established a name for reliability.

Korea has many enemies. North Korea is a constant threat and maintains a relentless propaganda war against the South. Terrorism is another weapon which North Korea has never hesitated to use. It has gone on down through the years. In February 1958 a plane flying from Pusan to Seoul was hijacked and made to fly to Pyongyang. In September 1967 there was two cases of trains north of Seoul being derailed by dynamite charges. In January 1968 a thirty-one-man North Korean commando unit actually succeeded in entering Seoul on a mission to assassinate the president, although that was foiled. In the same month, the world's attention was again focused on

Korea when the US intelligence ship *Pueblo* was forced into the northern port of Wonsan. That made the headlines for many weeks, and the brainwashing and treatment of the captured crew horrified the West. The incidents continue as a regular part of life in South Korea, with the disappearance on 29th November 1987 of a Korean Air Lines Boeing 707 with 115 people on board during a Baghdad-Seoul flight, which many think was linked with a terrorist bomb planted on board by North Korean agents operating from Japan.

The election in December 1987 is now history. Just what sort of a president Roh Tae Woo will prove himself, only time will tell. He has promised to break with Korea's corrupt past. The wrangling as to whether the voting was rigged will probably continue and the full truth never be known. The Christians I talked to before the election felt that there was little to choose between the candidates. It was not that Christians generally were for or against any of the candidates; what they were most definitely wanting was more democratisation and a government free from corruption. There was, they felt, probably some ballot rigging, but perhaps not as much as was feared because of the vigilence of the electorate and the media, and perhaps not enough to influence the result as much as did the fact that the opposition candidates could not find it in themselves to unite to provide a single opposition. After it was all over, Kim Dae Jung said that he was ashamed of his role in splitting the vote, as did the other candidate, Kim Young Sam.

The Korean church views the staging of the Olympics as an honour for the nation, but above all as another chance for sharing Christ with the world. It should always be borne in mind that although the nation is now divided into two separate states, the Koreans in both North and South are essentially one people and have been so for thousands of years. The factor that has made the principal difference between them is Christianity. Although the

South is not by any means a totally Christian nation, the North is fully communist and therefore the product of that teaching. But Christianity has had a tremendous influence for good in South Korea. It has contributed both politically and socially to the nation. The aim of Christians has been well expressed by the famous Dr Han Kyung-Chik, the pastor emeritus of Young Nak Presbyterian Church:

> We should pray earnestly, work harder, and be willing to give our lives to achieve true democracy in this land. We desire that freedom, equality, and a high respect of human rights will be practised and enjoyed by all people and that our nation will prosper.

This noted man of God acknowledges that there are too many fights and divisions among the churches, but points out that such divisions are not always negative: often both churches prosper, 'because God's grace works even through human weakness'. Korea is blessed with among the highest number of theological seminaries anywhere in the world. The standard of training for the ministry is one of the secrets of the growth and quality of the Korean church.

Taking everything into account and noting the present numerical strength and spiritual vitality of the Korean church, I trust that it can be agreed that Korea is a miracle indeed among the nations of the world today, a witness to the living God and his Christ.

I can think of no better way to conclude this book than with some more stirring words from Dr Han Kyung-Chik, penned on the occasion of the Protestant centenary in Korea:

> The reason God placed us in this land at this time is to evangelise our nation first, then North Korea, and then the whole world. We must recommit ourselves to the Lord with a new devotion, greater effort, and willing spirit of sacrifice to fulfil this great task.

Bibliography

A History of the Church in Korea Allen D Clark. The Christian Literature Society of Korea, Seoul, Korea. 1986 Edition.

The History of Protestant Missions in Korea 1832–1910 Lak-Geoon George Paik. Yonsei University Press, Seoul, Korea. 3rd Edition 1980.

Korea Church Growth Explosion (Centennial of the Protestant Church 1884–1984). Editors: Ro Bong-Rin and Marlin L Nelson. Asia Theological Association, Taichung, Taiwan, R O C and Word of Life Press, Seoul, Korea.

Wildfire: Church Growth in Korea Roy E Shearer. William B Eerdmans Publishing Company, Grand Rapids, Michigan.

Korea: The Best Kept Secret in Asia Tourist Information Centre, Seoul, Korea. (1985 Edition).

The Korean War Max Hastings. Michael Joseph Ltd, London 1987.

Korea Patterns Paul S Crane. Published for the Royal Asiatic Society by Kwangjin Publishing Co (4th edition, revised 1978).

Korea, New Pearl of the Orient. Korea National Tourism Corporation, S. Korea.

Church Growth Manual No. 1 (1987) Church Growth International, Korea.

Dream Your Way to Success Nell L Kennedy. Logos International, Plainfield, New Jersey, 07060 (1980).

Suffering . . . Why Me? Paul Yonggi Cho. Bridge Publishing, Inc, USA (1986).

Successful Living Paul Yonggi Cho. Youngan Publishing Co 1–20 Yoido dong, Yongdeungpo-ku, Seoul Korea (1976).

Solving Life's Problems Dr Paul Yonggi Cho. Logos International, Plainfield, New Jersey (1980).

The Fourth Dimension (Vol 1) Dr Paul Yonggi Cho. Logos International, Plainfield, New Jersey 1979.

The Fourth Dimension (Vol 2) Dr. Paul Yonggi Cho with R Whitney Manzano, Bridge Publishing, Inc USA (1983).

Understanding Church Growth Donald A McGavran. William B Eerdmans, Grand Rapids, Michigan (1982 Edition).

Prayer: Key to Revival Dr Paul Yonggi Cho with R Whitney Manzano. Word (UK) Ltd, Herts (1985).

Successful Home Cell Groups Dr Paul Yonggi Cho with Harold Hostetler. Logos International, Plainfield, New Jersey (1981).

Awakening in Asia Bailey Marks with Shirley McWhinney. Here's Life Inc, PO Box 1576, San Bernardino, CA 92402 (1981).

Home Group Cell System Church Growth International, Yoido, PO Box 7, Seoul 150, Korea (1987).

The Flaming Tongue J Edwin Orr. Moody Press, Chicago (1973).

God Can Do It Here! Eileen Vincent. Marshall Morgan and Scott (1982).

The Korean Revival Rene Monod. Hodder & Stoughton, London (1971).

Christianity in a Revolutionary Age, Vol 5.

A History of the Expansion of Christianity Vol 6.

A History of the Expansion of Christianity Vol 7.

A History of the Expansion of Christianity Vol 7. All by

Kenneth Scott Latourette. The Paternoster Press, Devon (1971 Edition).

More Than Numbers Dr Paul Yonggi Cho with R Whitney Manzano. UK Edition published by Bridge Publishing (UK) Gwent.

Operation World P J Johnstone. STL Publications, PO Box 48, Bromley, Kent (1978).

Korean Miracles Rev Jashil Choi. Seoul Book Publishing Company, Yoido PO Box 144, Seoul, Korea (1978).

China Miracle

by Arthur Wallis

Amazing growth through persecution
—Supernatural healings and other miracles
—A hunger for God and a lifestyle that
comes straight from the pages of the
New Testament.

These are some of the signs that are being reported from
the house churches in China. Arthur Wallis, who has
recently visited that land to see some of the churches for
himself, here presents us with an inspiring account of
what God is doing.

Starting with a clear and helpful historical survey, he
goes on to show that the church in China has vital
lessons to teach us here in the West. Above all we see a
church that lives in the power of the cross, determined to
remain faithful to her Lord no matter how tough the
opposition or how long the road to freedom.

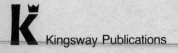

Kingsway Publications

Where the Brave Dare not Go

by Lela Gilbert

Russia—Africa—the Middle East...nowhere is too far for Irish-born Ray Barnett. And nowhere is too dangerous.

Many might feel that Christians persecuted in other lands are too remote to be within our reach. What can we do to help? The life of this remarkable man is guaranteed to silence such a question. Ray Barnett has seen answers to prayer that have defied governments, outwitted politicians and outflanked military regimes.

And through it all, he has been ready...ready to go anywhere, any time, when that unmistakable voice has sounded in his heart: 'Go now; there's something you can do'.

RAY BARNETT is President of Friends in the West, an organization dedicated to the release of oppressed Christians throughout the world. LELA GILBERT is also involved in the work, and a freelance writer.

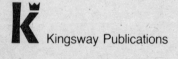

Kingsway Publications

Is That Really You, Lord?

by Loren Cunningham

As a young man, Loren Cunningham was given a startling vision of waves of young people moving out across the continents, spreading the gospel to a needy and rebellious world.

What did the vision mean? Was it telling him about the future? Was it from God?

In the birth of Youth With a Mission we see how hearing the voice of God can lead to great blessing if we are ready to obey Him in complete trust. As we see how God prepared Loren to tap the energies of young people for the gospel, we are encouraged to look for more of God's supernatural guidance in our own lives.

Loren Cunningham is Director of Youth With a Mission. He lives in Hawaii with his wife and two children. Janice Rogers is Loren's sister and a professional writer.

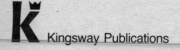

Kingsway Publications

C T Studd And Priscilla

by Eileen Vincent

A new biography of the pioneering missionaries.

What could cause a wealthy young man to give away his cricketing fame and personal fortune, and then bury himself in the depths of China? What was it that led him and his courageous wife on to India, four young daughters in tow?

Charles and Priscilla Studd: a man and woman who refused to deal in half measures. Controversial radicals in their day, they leave an inspiring example for all those who share the vision of a world-wide church and total allegiance to Christ.

Eileen Vincent takes us through the dramatic events of the lives of these great pioneers, taking into account personal correspondence not available to previous biographers. She writes not for the sake of history, but to reawaken in believers today an all-out passion for the evangelisation of people everywhere who do not know the love of Christ.

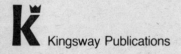

Kingsway Publications

Blood Brothers

by Elias Chacour *with David Hazard*

'The Jews and Palestinians are brothers, blood brothers,' said
father. 'We share the same father—Abraham—and the same
God. We must never forget that.'

Despite his father's words of peace, Elias Chacour sensed even
as a child that enmity and mistrust were not so easily overcome.

Once Christian and Jew had shared the simple things of life
together. But 1948 changed all that. The Zionists came, and
almost a million Palestinians were made homeless. An exile in
his own land, Elias faced the horrors of violence when tens of
thousands lost their lives.

Then his father, his brother, and most of the village men
disappeared.

In the years that followed, Elias struggled to find a way of peace
that would avoid violence and yet accomplish more than his
father's passive attitude. Then, just as he was about to begin a
quiet life of service to the church, he received a new and
dangerous calling that would take him right through the
world's most bitter conflict.

A way of hope and reconciliation beckoned.

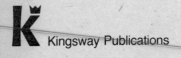

Kingsway Publications